Praise f

8 great dates about best friends and mean girls
from moms who have completed them...

"[The dates] were God-willed. You would be amazed at
how God worked in our lives through them."

Melissa

❀

"I love spending time with my daughter and having Secret Keeper Girl dates with
her makes our time together even more special. What's great about each date is that
they focus on different aspects of friendship—something I wasn't taught as a girl."

Natalie

❀

"My favorite date was the one with Dad. I just loved to see the girls' faces
light up when he answered questions about them and reaffirmed their inner
beauty and told of the wonderful things that God has planned for them...I am
keeping this kit to reuse with our younger daughter when she is older. Looking
forward to having great times of fun and discussion with her as well!"

Tarah

❀

"We have a small group at church doing these dates together. I think we have
all enjoyed them—it's hard to say which I like most! My daughter doesn't have
any siblings so I think she enjoyed borrowing a sister and ding-dong-ditching.
We actually did it a couple more times! Loved the whole thing, though!"

Tamara

❀

LOVED THEM!

Daneen

❀

"The date on mean girls was the most memorable one for my daughter. After
we got home from the mall challenge that taught us how love is 'slow to
boil,' she was so convicted about putting pressure on friends, she just cried
and cried. I told her this was GREAT news because if she wasn't convicted
then no change would happen. God loves it when we want to grow!"

Christi

❀

"The dates are awesome! During the shopping challenge date, I stood back to see what she would pick. I was amazed…at one point she held her arm out of the curtain saying, 'Return this dress—it isn't modest.' It helped me know she was starting to change, and I wouldn't have noticed if not for the date!"

Tessy

❀

"As a child of a single mom who tried to be both 'mother and father,' there is so much I did not learn growing up that I am now trying to instill in my daughters. SKG's 8 great dates have forced us to go out regularly and talk about all the things I never heard as a child…[these dates] are a tool to use to start the conversations with our daughters, and for that I am thankful!"

Barb

❀

"We did the dates and loved them! My daughter still implements the bod squad rules and I truly think her view on modesty and purity was developed with the help of this kit!"

Marji

❀

"We enjoyed it very much. Love the memorization of the 'love chapter' (1 Corinthians 13). It was great to witness our connection grow and evolve, and my daughter would agree."

Cindy

❀

8 Great Dates

Talking
with Your
Daughter
About

Best
Friends
AND Mean
girls

CREATOR OF
DANNAH GRESH
SECRET KEEPER GIRL

HARVEST HOUSE PUBLISHERS
EUGENE, OREGON

Interior photos: pages 21,24,27,89,100,161,172-174,181, and 188 by Steve Tressler; all others © Jupiter Images.

Interior character illustrations: page 129 by Andy Mylin; all others © Jupiter Images.

Cover by www.DesignByJulia.com, Woodland Park, Colorado

Interior design by Harvest House Publishers

TALKING WITH YOUR DAUGHTER ABOUT BEST FRIENDS AND MEAN GIRLS
Copyright © 2008, 2013 by Dannah Gresh
Published by Harvest House Publishers
Eugene, Oregon 97402
www.harvesthousepublishers.com

Library of Congress Cataloging-in-Publication Data
    Gresh, Dannah.
    Talking with your daughter about best friends and mean girls / Dannah Gresh.
        pages cm
    ISBN 978-0-7369-5529-4 (pbk.)
    ISBN 978-0-7369-5530-0 (eBook)
    1. Mothers and daughters—Religious aspects—Christianity. 2. Friendship—Religious aspects—Christianity. I. Title.
    BV4529.18.G743 2013
    241'.676208342—dc23
                                                                      2012047323

          13 14 15 16 17 18 19 20 21 /VP-JH/ 10 9 8 7 6 5 4 3 2 1

To my mother, Kay Barker

"Look…and be astounded.
For I am doing a work in your days
that you would not believe if told."
—Habakkuk 1:5

Acknowledgments

A Big SKG Squeeze to...

My dear friends at Harvest House, including LaRae Weikert, Terry Glaspey, Paul Gossard, Christianne Debysingh, Barb Sherrill, and the whole crew. How tenured this faithful team is, and how very grateful I am that you see the value of the Secret Keeper Girl message. (Don't forget Terry the next time you stop for lunch, LaRae!)

And thanks to The Resource Agency/Mike Keil, who introduced me to my friends at Harvest House.

BarlowGirl—Rebecca, Alyssa, and Lauren—jumped in to share secrets about friendship on the SKG kit audio downloads. There are few women who have come through the contemporary Christian music scene who I respect more. While recording and touring, they lived out the principles of a Secret Keeper Girl—modesty, purity, true beauty, and faithful friendship. Their stories are as fun and relevant today as when they were on tour.

Kelly (Witte) Nebel served as my research assistant for this project. *Jacqueline Gardner* revised the edition you hold in your hand. They are big book geeks just like me!

I could never write these books without my team at Pure Freedom holding all things together. Eileen King leads that team and is a great friend.

The biggest squeeze of all goes to my main squeeze, Bob. He had the vision for Secret Keeper and then to add the "girl" to it.

Thank You, Lord, for these friends!

I am forever in His Great Love.

—*Dannah*

Contents

Hi, Friend—

In your hand is one of the easiest-to-use resources you'll ever find. Let me give you a few key pointers about how to find things in this book. (In just a few pages, I'll explain how to use it and how to plan your mom-daughter dates.) But here's a quick look at what you'll see inside. (If you're an SKG—Secret Keeper Girl—pro who is familiar with our 8 Great Dates kits, you can fast-forward past this part!)

Part 1: Getting to Know Each Other. This is a hearty "hello" and "welcome" to Secret Keeper Girl. The first two chapters contain some self-reflection on our own quest for true friendship as moms, and then a dose of truth about the relationship culture your daughter is growing up in. Skim them if you want, but don't skip the third chapter. It tells you how to use the book!

Part 2: 8 Great Dates. Here they are in all their glory—the Secret Keeper Girl 8 Great Dates that teach your daughter about best friends and mean girls! Glance through them and you'll see that each one is easy to use...and very fun. (What mom wouldn't want to go on a shopping spree with her daughter?)

Part 3: Devotions and Other Good Stuff. This section is full of things you'll refer to as needed. Don't worry—I'll let you know when you need to dive in. The first part is the Secret Keeper Girl Devotions. You'll use these fantastic daily devotions after date #7, and I'll explain how at that point. The next section contains some frequently asked questions. I added this as moms wrote in with their most perplexing problems about best friends and mean girls. Finally, you'll find the Girl Gab pullouts for your daughter. These are similar to the Girl Gab pages you'll find in part two—8 Great Dates. They're perforated so you can pull them out and give them to your daughter.

Enjoy!

Dannah

Part 1

Getting to Know Each Other

Chapter One

A Mother's Relationships

H ere we are.
   You and I.

How ya been?

If I could take a pulse on your relationships right now, how would you fare? Is the heartbeat of friendship in your life strong and steady?

Or would you have to confess you have a little clogging of the arteries in that department?

Nearly comatose?

Or, worse yet, is there carnage all through your life because relationships have been a difficult business for you?

I have to confess that there's a little carnage in my path right now. That's not very common for me. It's been a painful year in the relationship department.

Trust was broken.

Accusations pierced my heart.

Territory was divided.

Tears continue to fall.

Can you identify? Just over a week ago, I was in bed having some kind of a seventh-grade pity party over all this friendship mess, when the thought actually ran through my head, "No one really likes me." (Yes, I fully acknowledge that I was reverting to adolescent angst.) Specifically I thought, "Laura doesn't really like me."

Now, my friend Laura *loves* me. I *know* she does. We've walked through some of the ugliest things together, rejoiced at miraculous victories in our lives, prayed our blonde heads off, and laughed equally as hard—usually at just how blonde we can be. I don't know why she happened to be the one who ran through my mind, but she was.

I begged the Lord to tell my heart Truth and let me sleep. I soon drifted off.

But the next morning he brought me full circle to Truth. You see, my friend Laura is deeply connected to the Lord, and he spoke to her in real time. When I got to my office, I found a handwritten note from her confirming her love for me. I could not believe it. What are the odds? Well, I'd never had a note from Laura in my office before!

I e-mailed her and confessed how wrecked my heart was feeling.

I kid you not…20 minutes later there was a knock on my door. And Laura's sweet face and very pregnant belly were soon filling the door frame.

"I thought maybe you could use a hug," she said.

My lips quivered and I felt so silly, but I leaned right into her round belly and received the embrace like a little child.

"Let me take you to lunch," she said.

Oh, how she rescued me that day!

Proverbs 17:17 tells us that "a friend loves at all times." Laura loved me when I wasn't very lovable. She listened to all my hurt and spoke strong rebukes to me because she knows that "faithful are the wounds of a friend" (Proverbs 27:6). I left lunch with homework to do in the relationship department assigned by my truth-filled friend, Laura.

Do you have *just one* friend like that?

If so, you are blessed!

If not, we've *got* to get you some, girl!

You may have picked up this Secret Keeper Girl kit with the intention of helping your daughter navigate through the murky waters of relationships, but I'm praying that it also helps you take the pulse of your own relationships. And to bring them into conformity with the heartbeat of our God!

Let's start with him, shall we?

Just stop for a moment and ask the precious Holy Spirit to make your heart receptive to the scriptural truth and encouragement in the pages ahead. After all, how can we teach our daughters to have healthy relationships if we've not learned how to have them ourselves?

"There is a friend who sticks closer than a brother" (Proverbs 18:24).

His name is Jesus.

Talk to him.

Now.

Chapter Two

Your Daughter's Relationships

I never really had sleepovers.

We had sleepovers—me and my mom!

I can still remember her perched on the edge of our basement stairs, that multishaded tan shag carpeting beneath her. We girls were all tucked into our sleeping bags in the dark, and the conversations began. Before I knew it, my mom was curled up right next to us answering questions about why boys are so noisy (they apparently just wanted our attention, but we shouldn't give them too much), what to do about the smelly girl in class (she was at our next sleepover), and how to handle the male science teacher who was always touching our legs when we went up to his desk (he never did again after that sleepover). As she talked with us well into the wee hours of the morning, I often found myself wondering if my girlfriends came to spend the night with me or with my mom. I knew that they loved her.

But I never minded. Not one bit.

I was proud of my mom.

I reveled in her sleepover advice.

Little did I know, she was teaching me the delicate art of relationships.

And oh, how important that was. A little girl's relationships are critical to her overall development. Little boys like relationships. Little girls *need* them.

Friends!

Your daughter's friends are becoming increasingly more important to her. Sixty-seven percent of tween girls—those aged 8 to 12—say that "having lots of friends" is among the top three factors that give them the most confidence. [1] As your daughter ages, you'll see an increase in talking and a definite increase in usage of social media like Facebook and online messaging. Don't be surprised if you're nagged because "everyone else" has a cell phone. She was created to communicate, so her relationships are going to be taking a top priority in her life!

Boy-Craziness!

Guys may become interesting to her, but she's not ready for relationships yet. Being in a dating relationship for six months or longer is a significant risk factor for early teen sexual activity. [2] Can you see why it might not be that "cute" for our 8- to 12-year-olds to be boy-crazy or have multiple boyfriends while they are still in the fourth grade? If she develops the pattern of "needing" a guy when she is eight or nine, she's going to be in many six-month relationships in her early teen years. That's not wise. Let's help her to slow down the boy-crazy train in her circle of friends.

Dad!

Her relationship with her daddy—or a father figure—is a literal lifeline. The *Chicago Sun-Times* reported that "reams of research show that girls who are close to their dads are less likely to be promiscuous, develop eating disorders, drop out of school or commit suicide." [3] A daddy's love keeps a girl emotionally stable. That could be a great challenge in your daughter's life depending on how and whether her daddy is involved in her life. Let me show you how to approach the issue so that you can make the daddy factor—no matter what your situation—good news.

Mom!

Her relationship with you is still one she treasures. Seventy-two percent of tween girls feel they can talk to their mom about anything. [4] And they do. Don't miss this, Mom. In just a few years (or months), she's going to start to feel a little different about that. (She may even act as if you've had a lobotomy!) Use this time when her heart is open to prepare her and train her. *This is the time to talk about friendships, boys, and other big issues*—while her heart is receptive to your wisdom.

What she learns about relationships now determines how she'll date, marry, and build a family—with a healthy God-directed plan or with a selfish, often self-destructive plan. It'll help her or hinder her in establishing a life purpose. Your discipleship in this area will equip her to be the heartbeat of God on this earth or train her to spread the carnage of broken relationships.

Teach her well, Mom.

Let me give you the tools to do it in eight easy-to-plan dates!

Chapter Three

How to Use
Talking with Your Daughter About Best Friends and Mean Girls

Since I wrote the original Secret Keeper Girl friendship kit, my precious Lexi has graduated high school and our second daughter, Autumn, whom we adopted from China, will soon be following in her footsteps. Both are 19 years old. *Wow!* I welcome times when they are willing to be alone with me and tell me the secrets of their hearts. It doesn't happen enough at this age, and I wish I'd have taken even more time to nestle Lexi in my arms when she was 8, 9, 10, 11, and 12. (Even though I rarely stopped squeezing her then!) I so treasure the moments we shared together when she was my *little* girl!

How to Be a "Connecting Mom"

One of the greatest factors in teaching your daughter about relationships and reducing high-risk teen behaviors like early sexual activity is parent-child connectedness. I've written an entire book for you just about how to become a "connecting mom." It's called *Six Ways to Keep the "Little" in Your Girl: Guiding Your Daughter from Her Tweens to Her Teens*, and it would be a fantastic companion tool for you as you begin connecting to your little girl on these 8 Great Dates.

What You'll Find in This Book

Each Secret Keeper Girl resource is packed with tools for you to have some of those mom-daughter moments with your precious girl. They are simple guides to plan eight fun dates for you and her to spend time together. In this kit, which is all about friendships, we'll explore key relationships and true love. Most dates will be approximately one-and-a-half hours long (excluding your planning and extra travel during the date). Be sure to bring a camera along for at least some of your dates so you have photos for the Secret Keeper Girl scrapbook you can create as an optional activity. (More on that later.) You may plan dates weekly or just spread them out and do them as you can schedule them into your life. Just don't let them get too far apart. Although each date will have a slightly different friendship focus and activity, they will all have the same "sections." Your date from start to finish will include the following:

SKG Prep Talk

The Prep Talk gives you a little challenge of your own and an overview of the date. It's best if you plan to read through this section at least *several* days in advance. That way you can make appointments or reservations, purchase supplies, or schedule specials guests into the date.

SKG Radio: 7-10 Minutes

There's one really cool part of these 8 Great Dates that requires just a touch of technical skill. (You can recruit someone to help if you are technically challenged. You'll only need help once.) Visit secretkeepergirl.com and download the free audio MP3s that accompany these dates. After you download them, you can either burn a CD for the CD player in your car, or just store them on your iPod or MP3 player so you can play them for your daughter on the way to and from the dates. The SKG radio moments really support your dates. My friends Alyssa, Rebecca, and Lauren Barlow and I will be right there "with" you to share a story and get your hearts thinking in the right direction for the upcoming activities. Can you do the dates without them? Probably, but they do add a lot of depth to your experience. Go ahead. Tackle technology!

SKG Challenge: 30-45 Minutes

This is the real fun! The challenge is what you'll do at your special destination. (Think sleepover, a shopping spree, and ding-dong-ditching the neighbors!) These are either object lessons or simply outright challenge assignments from which you can learn.

SKG Girl Gab: 15-25 Minutes (with optional scrap-booking afterward)

This is major girl talk! You and your daughter will have similar pages, except she'll use the Girl Gab pullout pages in the back. These may include reading and discussing Bible verses or completing evaluations or taking inventories. You'll also need one fun and funky scrapbook for your daughter. A simple 99-cent spiral-bound book will work, or you can go all out and visit a craft store like Michaels for something with glitz and glitter. (If you really dislike scrapbooking, you can skip that altogether. The important part is that you do the Girl Gab pullout pages.) The main purpose of the scrapbook will be to store your Girl Gab pullouts after you've filled in the blanks on your date. Later on, you can also add photos of the dates and other memorabilia like tickets or receipts. But don't do your fun scrapbooking as a part of your date time. Stick to the simple task of filling out the Girl Gab pages supplied at the back of this book.

Budget Crunchers

If money is a big concern, relax! In the few dates that may be more expensive, I'll offer you tips on how to do them economically. Keep in mind that the budget option may require more time and planning.

Here's an overview of
your dates and all the fun to come!

Date #1:

True Friendship in God's Eyes

Challenge activity: A slumber party
Key verse: 1 Corinthians 14:1
Key thought: A Secret Keeper Girl pursues love.
Suggested challenge setting: Your house, a hotel
with a pool, a cozy cabin, or a tent in the woods

Date #2:

Friendship with My Neighbor

Challenge activity: Commit an act of kindness
Key verses: 1 Corinthians 13:1-3
Key thought: True love overflows with acts of kindness.
Suggested challenge setting: Anyplace where
you can commit an unexpected act of kindness
for someone you don't know, such as a county
fair, street corner, neighborhood, or city park

Date #3:

Friendship with Mean Girlz

Challenge activity: A shopping spree
Key verses: 1 Corinthians 13:4-6
Key thought: True love is patient, even with mean girlz.
Suggested challenge setting: A local mall

Date #4:

Friendship with My BFF
Challenge activity: Create a BFF scrapbook
Key verse: 1 Corinthians 13:7a
Key thought: Real love doesn't gossip.
Suggested challenge setting: A favorite
place to hang out with your BFF

Date #5:

Friendship with My Parents
Challenge activity: A date with Dad and
some even furrier creatures
Key verse: 1 Corinthians 13:7b
Key thought: True love trusts.
Suggested challenge setting: A farm, pet store, or a zoo

Date #6:

Friendship with My Siblings
Challenge activity: Ding-dong-ditch someone
Key verse: 1 Corinthians 13:7c
Key thought: True love hopes for the best in someone.
Suggested challenge setting: Your kitchen and the
front door of someone you know won't mind

Date #7:
Friendship with God

Challenge activity: A quiet encounter with God

Key verses: 1 Corinthians 13:8-11

Key thought: God is our only source of unfailing love.

Suggested challenge setting: Any place of solitude, such as a forest, a snowy mountain, the ocean, or even a candlelit bubble bath

Date #8:
Friendship with Boyz

Challenge activity: To play like the boyz

Key verses: 1 Corinthians 13:12-13

Key thought: True love pursues one lifelong relationship.

Suggested challenge setting: A laser-tag arena, a paintball field, or a go-kart track

Small-Group Alternative

This SKG kit is all about friendship, so it really would be fitting to do all of the dates as a small group. Date #1 suggests that you have up to eight of your daughter's friends *and* their mothers on hand for the fun. It's a great kickoff to invite them to do all of the 8 Great Dates with you. *You'll always have Girl Gab time all alone with your daughter*, but you'll also be teaching her friends how to be true friends as you teach her. The results could be fantastic: no more mean girls, no more getting left out, no more jealousy! Anyway, you and a few moms can do this together. I'll leave it up to you to decide how to do that. Here are some ideas:

1. Do all the dates together. Take turns planning and leading. If you do it with a group of eight mother-daughter pairs, you'll have to invest the time into planning only one date. This will make the load lighter and heighten the fun!

2. Do dates #1 and #8 together. Just keep tabs on each other in the middle dates, but use the first and last dates as a kickoff and a celebration of your completion.

3. Do dates #1, #4, and #8 together. These dates most lend themselves to having friends on hand to talk with and have fun with. For date #4, you'll be making a scrapbook page of friendship. You can all do your own page, but enjoy the conversation if you do it in the same room, computer lab, or coffee shop!

If you do the dates with a small group, be sure to get the moms together for lunch now and then to update and encourage one another. It might even be a great chance for you to develop your own true friendships!

SKG Radio: 3-4 Minutes

On your way home, just pop your CD or MP3 player back on for a special surprise. BarlowGirl will share their own secret moments of struggling with relationships, including those with friends, parents, and boyz!

SKG Driveway Prayer: 3-5 Minutes

You'll wrap up each great date with an intimate prayer in your driveway. Don't skip this vital time of growing closer through the power of God's presence. Your book will give you an idea of what you might pray, but feel free to go in whatever direction God leads you for this time.

Well, that's pretty much it.

Ready to start planning your first date?

Part 2

8 Great Dates

True Friendship in God's Eyes

Challenge activity:
A slumber party

Key verse: 1 Corinthians 14:1

Key thought: A Secret Keeper Girl pursues love.

Suggested challenge setting: Your house, a hotel with a pool, a cozy cabin, or a tent in the woods

SKG Prep Talk

Fifty-six percent of girls say they look to close friends as their role models. [5] But you already knew that, didn't you? Your daughter is most likely a social butterfly who thrives on relationship and whose precious, tender wings wilt when she's "left out." Most girls are molded by their friendship experiences to a great degree.

That begs the question: Should you—or should you not— help your daughter choose her friends? Let's ask the girls what they think. According to a survey of 8- to 12-year-old girls conducted by *Discovery Girls* magazine,

- 12 percent say "yes"
- 67 percent say "no"
- 21 percent say "it depends"[6]

So, most girls would say that you *shouldn't* help them choose their friends. (You are blessed if you have one who is in that wise 12 percent. Don't forget to thank her!)

The Bible teaches strongly that we are to train up our children in the way they should go, and it equally encourages us to realize that "whoever walks with the wise becomes wise" (Proverbs 13:20). It makes clear sense to me that we ought to be spending these years of our daughters' lives training them to choose wise friends.

Let's get—or stay—involved!

Prep Talk with God

Take a moment to pray. Pray that God would help you to have a strong commitment to helping your daughter choose wise friends. Pray that her heart would be open to your involvement. Specifically ask the Lord which of her current friendships you should help her to pursue. Write the names of those girls and their moms below. Praise God for these friendships.

1.   5.

2.   6.

3.   7.

4.   8.

Slumber Party SKG Style!

Subject: Pursuing love

Setting options: Your house, a hotel with a pool, a cozy cabin, or a tent in the woods

Materials you'll need at your destination:

- One die (that's one of a pair of dice!)
- Pens
- A sheet of paper for each mother and each daughter
- One white pillowcase for each daughter
- One printed iron-on SKG logo from www.secret keepergirl.com for each daughter (optional)
- Fabric markers
- This book
- Your Bibles

This date will kick off your lessons in true love. Who better to do that with than your daughter's friends? If you've done 8 Great Dates on true beauty, cool fashion, and modesty, then you know that I like to call your daughter's good, wise, accountability-lending friends the Bod Squad! Tonight, you'll be collecting her Bod Squad for a great sleepover and some truth-filled conversation. Your actual SKG date time will take about one-and-a-half hours of the sleepover. The rest is yours to be creative with. You can be as simple or as extravagant as you want to be with your planning.

SKG Radio:
7-10 Minutes

Play "Date #1: Pursuing Love" as you drive to your destination.

Note: If you are driving to a hotel or mountain cabin and can all ride together, listen as a group. If you are all arriving separately at your location and each mom has her own SKG kit, ask each to listen on their own as they drive. As a last resort, you can play it at the beginning of your slumber party once everyone has arrived.

SKG Challenge:
30-45 Minutes

We're going to do two seemingly unconnected activities, but they'll fit together when we begin to talk through them in the teaching time. Stick with me.

1. Sixes. Let's start with one of my family's favorite games: sixes. The goal is to be the first person to write the numbers 1 through 100 on her sheet of paper. The only catch is that there is only one pen for everyone to share.

To play, you just need the die (the singular form of "dice"), one pen, and a sheet of paper for each person at the party. Sit at a table. Each person will take turns rolling the die. When someone rolls a 6, they grab the pen and start writing the numbers 1 through 100 on their sheet of paper. They write furiously until someone else rolls a 6, at which time they must relinquish the pen. The first person to write all of the numbers 1 through 100 wins! (When you reclaim the pen, you pick up at whatever number you wrote the last time you had it.) Encourage the girls to be fast, and you'll see how fun it can be after just one round. It gets aggressive! (You'll soon be addicted to this game, and it fits in your pocket for family trips and church events!) Play several rounds before moving on to activity number two.

2. Love-fest memory pillows. Next, you'll create a sleepover memory that's inexpensive but very powerful. Each girl will get one white pillowcase with the SKG logo ironed onto it (optional) or just a white pillowcase. Instruct the girls to create a border for the pillowcase using the fabric markers, each one making sure to include her name in her favorite big letters. As they begin, remind them to decorate only the border and leave most of the middle empty.

SKG-Style Pillowcases

Want a really fun way to get the pillowcase started SKG style? Go to www.secretkeepergirl.com and find the 8 Great Dates downloads page. You'll find a downloadable SKG logo you can print onto Avery brand iron-on paper from most printers. It also creates a corner border for your girls' pillowcases. They just need to add in their name.

After the girls have completed their border, invite them to pass their pillowcase to the person on their right. Ask each girl to close her eyes and pray about how God sees the person whose pillowcase is in front of them and to think about what good qualities they see in that person. Then, each will draw something that represents what they think God sees or what they see. For example, if a girl thinks this person is the life of the party and is always loving, she might draw a heart bursting with confetti. If she thinks this person is super strong and always someone she can lean on, she might draw a tall tree with a thick trunk. Relax! It'll come naturally. Girls love doodling! The key is that what they draw must have meaning. Make sure each girl has a quick moment to sign her name beside her art before she passes it on to the next person. Keep the pillowcases moving until they make it back to their owner.

Now the real fun begins! As each girl holds up her pillowcase, have her friends verbally share why they drew what they drew. I have a friend who likes to call this a love fest! It's great to see how special each girl feels when she hears the affirming things her friends say about her.

SKG Girl Gab:
15-25 Minutes

You may split up into mom and daughter pairs for this part of the conversation if you all have books or you may do it as a group discussion with just you leading. Here's a suggested conversation to get you started.

Mom: Both of those activities were fun, weren't they?

Daughter: (Hopefully she'll agree!)

Mom: Sixes was really crazy. As we ripped that pen from each other's hands and greedily tried to be the first one to get to 100, I had a thought—"What if that's how we spent all of our time with our friends—selfishly grabbing for things and being competitive?"

Daughter: (She may say that it wouldn't be a good way to build friendships.)

Mom: But making the pillowcases was totally the opposite, wasn't it? You were thinking of how to encourage and lift up your friends. How did it make you feel when you heard what your friends had to say about you?

Daughter: (She will probably indicate that she was encouraged.)

Mom: Like Dannah [pronounced like "Hannah"] said on our audio teaching, God commands you and me to "pursue love." True love must be at the heart of every Secret Keeper Girl's friendships. I saw you and your friends showing true love while you made those pillowcases.

I wonder, if we analyzed our friendships—mine, ours, yours—which activity would we best reflect? The one where we're grabbing for what we can get or the one where we're giving out love? I'll go first. I think that a lot of times, I'm pursuing real love especially when I _____. But I've got to admit that it's more like I'm playing that game of sixes when I _____. Which are you?

Daughter: (Could vary. She may name a specific friendship that's more like the sixes game and one that's more like real love. Be prepared to simply direct the conversation for a few minutes. Let her express her thoughts about what you've just said.)

Mom: Well, I know I'd rather be pursing love like God commands me to in my friendships, but sometimes I need to be reminded of where I'm falling short. With this Secret Keeper Girl book, you and I are both going to learn how to do that!

This will be the first time to present your daughter with her new scrapbook (if you're planning to do that). You might want to gift-wrap it or put it in a gift bag with a fuzzy pen and some candy, along with her first page from the Girl Gab pages, which you'll find at the end of this book. All you need to do is pull them out and prepare to use them. Your own Girl Gab page is right here. If you want to have party favors at your SKG-Style Slumber Party, you can present them now.

During each Girl Gab time, you'll let your daughter read the little introduction and fill in the blank for her key thought. Help her if she needs it. These are often tucked pretty deeply into the SKG audio teaching. You'll have the answers on your pages (unless the answers are subjective).

Then, ask her to proceed to the meat of today's Girl Gab. For this date, you'll ask her to take the Love Meter test and then map herself on it. You'll fill yours out too. Give each other a few minutes and then use the rest of your time to discuss the Love Meter. This is all about getting her to gab her heart out so you can hear what's in it!

Your daughter's Girl Gab for this date is on page 155.

Mom Notes:

. . . .

. . . .

. . . .

. . . .

Budget Cruncher:

1. Of course, this date would be a blast at a hotel with a pool. If you put four in a room and divide the costs, you may find some Internet specials that break the cost down to only $30 to $50 per mother-daughter pair. For snacks, just some chips and soda will do since the pool is the key feature. A cabin may be even cheaper, especially if you know some friends who would let you use theirs for free!

2. For a less expensive option, host the night at a campground. Just $10 to $20 will usually get you a clean, safe place to pitch your tent. Of course, this option is also more work and you'll need a tent, sleeping bags, firewood, and so on. Make a list and go for it if this sounds fun to you. (But run like the plague if it doesn't. Remember, the key to these dates is to enjoy them!)

3. If you're in need of the very least expensive way to do this date, invite the girls and moms to your house after dinner on a Friday night. Ask each pair to bring a snack to share, along with a blank white pillowcase. Just provide the napkins and drinks and you can pull off the entire night for as little as $10 to $20! While this isn't the most unique experience, it'll still be very memorable.

Date #1: True Friendship in God's Eyes

Girl Gab

Welcome to SKG! That stands for Secret Keeper Girl, and I'm hoping you'll want to be one if you aren't already. If you did the 8 Great Dates on true beauty, cool fashion, and modesty, you know that a Secret Keeper Girl is *a masterpiece created by God*. That's the core of what and who you are! But…just how does a masterpiece created by God live and interact with all of God's other great masterpieces, like your mom, dad, BFFs, and boyz? That's what we're going to discover during these eight great dates! Earlier I introduced an important quality that's in every SKG. Do you recall what that is?

A Secret Keeper Girl pursues (true love).

"Pursue love."
1 Corinthians 14:1 NASB

❋ ❋ ❋

Love Meter

Okay, let's take girl talk to a new level. It's called Girl Gab. So, are your friendships more like that game of sixes or more like that sweet SKG-Style Memory Pillow experience? Let's find out by taking this Love Meter test.

Read the following scenarios and decide where they'd rank on the Love Meter.

 Your friend meets someone new at camp, you decide it's not fair that she doesn't spend all her time with you, and you give her the silent treatment the rest of the week.

 You see your friend out riding her bike with the new girl in the neighborhood. The next day on the bus, you ask your friend how you can encourage the new girl too.

 It's summer break and things in the neighborhood aren't going so well. It seems that with three of you living on the same street, there's always one too many. You decide you're only going to hang with one friend at a time because you're tired of the drama.

 Someone in class just said something terrible about your BFF. You quickly jump in to set the record straight. No one is going to say something bad about your friend!

 It's Friday and you told one friend she could ride the bus home with you after school, but a better offer has come up. You decide to go with friend number two to the movies instead.

 Your friend just got a really bad haircut and she's crying her eyes out. You tell her truthfully that you really loved it longer but she's always adorable in your book. You remind her that it'll grow back.

The girl two doors down just told you her scariest secret last night: She thinks her mom and dad are getting divorced. You can't help yourself. You tell the girls at school during lunch break.

 You didn't mean to do it, but you hurt the feelings of one of your classmates. You write her a note to apologize.

Okay, now that you've taken a good look at some fictional scenarios, let's take it up a notch.

Write one real-life scenario where you showed the kind of love that makes a friendship run on a full tank:

. . . .

. . . .

. . . .

. . . .

Now, write one scenario where you have to confess that you drained the Love Meter big-time:

. . . .

. . . .

. . . .

. . . .

If you were to put a great big star on the place where the needle on your Love Meter generally points, where would it be? Mark that spot with a star.

Now, write one idea that can help you be more consistent in operating on full:

(Mother's example: I gave myself a 3, because I realize that I need to control my tongue more. I want my friends to know that their secrets are safe with me. So, I'm making it a goal to not talk about someone unless they are there.)

(Daughter's example: I need to be less jealous when my friends have another friend around. From now on, I'm going to try to be happy when I see my friend enjoying someone else. That's how I'd want her to be for me.)

. . . .

. . . .

. . . .

. . . .

Moms, after you've had time to encourage your daughter in the goals she's set, tell her how proud you are of her.

SKG Radio:
3-4 Minutes

Play your audio files as you go home to hear what BarlowGirl has to say about pursuing true love!

As you arrive home (or tidy up after everyone leaves), spend a few minutes praying about the goals you've set concerning friendship.

SKG Driveway Prayer:
3-5 Minutes

Friendship with My Neighbor

Challenge activity:
Commit an act of kindness

Key verses: 1 Corinthians 13:1-3

Key thought: True love overflows with acts of kindness.

Suggested challenge setting: Anyplace where you can commit an unexpected act of kindness for someone you don't know, such as a county fair, street corner, neighborhood, or city park

SKG Prep Talk

I'm surprised every time I see it.

The open spirit.

Last week Lexi started volunteering at a preschool to give weary workers some rest. She came home with what I can only call an open spirit. It's kind of inexplicable if you've never seen it before, but I imagine you have. It's what happens to your "what-about-*me*" kid (who got the "what-about-*me*" mentality by natural, generational inheritance) when he or she discovers the joy of existing in a "what-about-*you*" place. There's a wonder that happens in them. As if they've stumbled onto something they were created for outside of text messaging, dance lessons, and their favorite Wii game. Some kind of satisfaction that doesn't exist in those things rises up and opens their spirits.

I saw it in Lexi when she passed out cold water to strangers on a hot summer day with her youth group.

I saw it in Robby when he came home with his brand-new sneakers stained because he'd spent the day picking up huge, muddy rocks for a local church.

I saw it in Autumn when she and I delivered a hot meal to a family who has no mom.

It's not how we live these days. We're much too busy keeping up with *American Idol* and *Dancing with the Stars* to take time for someone else, but oh, it feels good when we get it.

Wanna have some fun?

Commit an act of kindness!

Prep Talk with God

Take a moment right now to present your own kindness to the Lord. Ask him to open your heart to love someone you don't even know and to make that love contagious to your daughter's heart.

Commit an Act of Kindness!

Subject: Friendship with my neighbor

Setting options: Anyplace where you can commit an unexpected act of kindness for someone you don't know, such as a county fair, street corner, neighborhood, or city park

Materials you'll need at your destination:

- Selection depending upon the act of kindness you select (see sidebar on page 52 for ideas)

- This book

- The phrase, "We just want to show God's love in a practical way" (read on!)

This date is all about learning that love is shown through acts of kindness, especially to what the Bible refers to as our neighbors—people we don't have much of a connection to other than proximity. Of course, acts of kindness without love have little meaning. It all begins with love. We are nothing without it.

So, I'm sending you out to hit the streets to actually *do* 1 Corinthians 13:1-3 by committing an act of kindness. Check out the sidebar on page 52 for ideas on how to plan yours. I suggest that you talk this over with your daughter ahead of time and let her be a part of deciding what exciting act of kindness you will commit!

On this date, you'll also begin the exciting challenge of memorizing all of 1 Corinthians 13, the "Love Chapter." Our teaching for all of the dates will come from this powerful passage.

What a lifelong treasure you will give to your daughter if you take the time to hide this passage in her heart!

SKG Radio:
7-9 Minutes

Play "Date #2: Love Overflows with Acts of Kindness" on your way to your random act of kindness location.

An act of kindness requires that you love someone that you don't even know—a "neighbor," but not the one who is your best friend. I want you to use this to teach your daughter about loving anyone she comes close to by mere geographical providence.

SKG Challenge:
30-45 Minutes

Your act of kindness should qualify in the following four areas.

It should be **random**. This means you don't know the people you bless with your kindness and you don't plan it way in advance. It's not something you are obligated to do, like baking cookies for a school bake sale or serving in the nursery. You're going to let God guide you to someone who needs his love and kindness today.

It's **active**. You have to get out there in the world and *do* something. Maybe it's raking leaves for someone you don't even know or handing out hot chocolate to the bus drivers in the school parking lot one cold winter afternoon.

It's **kind**. You want to knock someone's socks off. And trust me, you will. Once when my son did a random act of kindness with his high school, a family they visited said they'd prayed just that morning, "Lord, if you are still in control, please show us in a tangible way." Little did my son and his friends know that the family whose door they would knock on had lost their father and husband only weeks earlier. They were having a particularly bad day. When three high-school boys showed up with cookies they'd baked to say, "We just wanted to say God loves you in a practical way," the mom of the house accused them of having a dead animal in the box! They assured her that they did not. Her heart melted as she opened the cookies, and it affirmed to the whole family that God was, in fact, watching over them. You have no idea what adventure is ahead on this date!

Finally, you simply say,

"We just wanted to show **God's Love** in a practical way."

Don't give any specific church or group credit. Don't mention Secret Keeper Girl! Don't give your family name credit. Just let God have it all.

Enjoy the fruit of watching your daughter's spirit open!

One important note: Don't just do this act without praying for the people you surprise. As you go through with your act of kindness, be sure to help your daughter notice any special needs evidenced by the way people appear or things that they say to you. You'll come back to those needs during Girl Gab time.

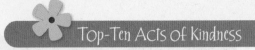

Top-Ten Acts of Kindness

Here are some great ideas to get your thoughts rolling.

10. Buy a dozen roses and hand them out one by one to people who pass you by on a street corner.

9. Bake a batch of cookies and package them nicely. Deliver them to several random homes.

8. Go out for ice cream or to Starbucks and pay for the people behind you.

7. Make a pot of hot chocolate or coffee and deliver Styrofoam cups full of it to all of the bus drivers that stop near your house.

6. Take a pitcher of lemonade out to a random construction site and refresh the workers.

5. Work with some other SKGs and offer a free car wash in a grocery-store parking lot. (This would take some setup ahead of time.)

4. Take a babysitting job, but refuse to accept the money.

3. Leave a bag of coins taped to a vending machine with a note that reads, *It's on me*.

2. Bake a homemade apple pie and deliver it to the staff of a nursing home with a note to encourage them.

1. Buy a case of bottled water, cool it, and hand it out at a city park or county fair on a hot day.

An act of kindness doesn't have to cost one penny! You can grab your manicure kit and nail polish and head to a nursing home. There you'll offer free treatments to any of the older ladies who want one. In the fall, you can rake leaves for someone. In the spring or summer, you can pull weeds. The point isn't to spend money, but to spread kindness.

Budget Cruncher:

Acts of Kindness Photo Contest

Hey, wanna inspire other SKGs across the nation? Why not post a photo of your act of kindness along with a brief story about what you did on the Secret Keeper Girl Facebook page?

SKG Girl Gab:
15-25 Minutes

Today's Girl Gab time will be spent talking about the great act of kindness you and your daugther just committed. We've provided some pages where your daughter can record her thoughts, paste photos, or draw pictures. Enjoy the conversation!

Your daughter's Girl Gab for this date is on page 159

Date #2: Friendship with My Neighbor

Girl Gab

On our first SKG date, that awesome SKG-Style Slumber Party, you discovered that at the root of all relationships must be true love. So, this week we begin a quest to discover just what true love looks like. It's not that feeling like butterflies in your tummy. No, it's not that at all! God's Word defines love, and it's going to take us seven dates to really explore his full definition. Along the way, we'll learn how to find new friends, handle the emotions of getting left out, stop jealousy, control our tongue, honor our parents—and even learn how to be friends with boyz. Best of all, we find all that advice in just one chapter of the Bible: 1 Corinthians 13!

Today, let's just focus on the first three verses.

> *"If I speak with the tongues of men and of angels, but do not have love, I have become a noisy gong or a clanging cymbal. If I have the gift of prophecy, and know all mysteries and all knowledge; and if I have all faith, so as to remove mountains, but do not have love, I am nothing. And if I give all my possessions to feed the poor, and if I surrender my body to be burned, but do not have love, it profits me nothing."*
> *1 Corinthians 13:1-3* NASB

According to 1 Corinthians 13:1-3 and our SKG audio teaching today, fill in this blank.

Real love overflows with (acts of kindness).

It's easy to be consumed with how love shows up in your family and in friendships. But if you have real love in your heart, you'll also love your neighbors. According to our SKG audio teaching, who is your neighbor?

(Anyone God decides I need to bump into today!)

If you are pursuing true love, you'll find yourself willing to go out and do extraordinary acts of kindness for people you don't even know. You'll be willing to get out from behind your Wii. You'll turn off the instant messaging. You'll forget the reruns of *Hannah Montana* that you've seen ten times, and you'll go out and act on the love God's put in your heart!

How did you and your mom commit an act of kindness today? Pretend you're preparing a newspaper article to report on it. Write your story below and begin with this sentence:

"An act of kindness was committed today at…"

. . . .

Where?

. . . .

When?

. . . .

Who?

. . . .

What?

. . . .

. . . .

Who did you meet along the way? Draw a picture of one to three people you met and then next to the pictures, write how you might pray for them with your mom. What special needs did you notice or did they tell you about?

Now, back to our key Bible verse. Not only does it mention that we need to do acts of kindness, but it says more. Look at it to fill in another couple of blanks.

If we do anything without (love) we are (nothing).

Hmm? I don't know about you, but I often do acts of kindness to get attention and to be applauded. It's really hard to do them just out of love. That's why today when you were out and about, I asked you to say, "I just want to show God's love in a practical way." Shining the glory on God goes a long way in stretching my heart to love.

There's another thing that helps—praying! You'll end your date tonight by praying. What will you pray about? Go back to your drawings of three people that you met. Write one idea of how you can pray for that person next to each one.

Now, remember to pray over the next few days for the people you met.

One more thing! You can join me in the huge but ultimately completely rewarding goal of memorizing the entire chapter of 1 Corinthians 13. You can start now by learning verses 1-3! I'll be doing it along with you.

SKG Radio:
3-4 Minutes

Pop your SKG audio lesson on to learn about how the sisters of BarlowGirl pray for people that they meet.

Using your daughter's idea from her journal, pray for the people you met today as you committed your acts of kindness. Take turns asking God to increase your love for them and to remind you to pray for them over the next few days.

SKG Driveway Prayer:

3-5 Minutes

Friendship with Mean Girlz

Challenge activity:
A shopping spree

Key verses: 1 Corinthians 13:4-6
Key thought: True love is patient, even with mean girlz.
Suggested challenge setting: A local mall

SKG Prep Talk

"That seat is saved!"

Words that too many of us have heard reverberate through her mind as she looks around at the glares of those who obviously don't want her to sit near them. The cloud of rejection settles thickly over her heart.

She's not in seventh grade—the height of relationship turmoil for most of us. She's in a PhD program. Her name is Rosalind Wiseman. And the constant catty rejection makes her want to quit.

She doesn't.

She first moves through it and then on to write *Queen Bees*

& *Wannabes*, the nonfiction bestseller that would become the basis for *Mean Girls*, the movie starring Lindsay Lohan.

Of course, Rosalind could have also been in second grade. The mean-girls mentality hits early and, apparently, can last long. You've probably seen it when your daughter gets "left out." (Or maybe yours is the one doing the leaving out.) The problem is that mean little girls grow up to be mean women! What they're doing now is just rehearsal for what their lives will look like.

What's your daughter rehearsing to be—the wounder or protector of hearts?

Prep Talk with God

Take a moment right now to confess any sin—old or much too fresh—in this area. Have you ever been a mean girl? A mean woman? Ask the Lord to cleanse you of any sin in this area. Or maybe you weren't the mean girl, but were the target of mean girls. Have you ever taken time to verbally pronounce forgiveness and ask for healing? If not, do that today. Plead with God to prepare you to be a good counselor for your daughter as she navigates through this mean-girl world.

Planning Date #3

A Fast-Paced Shopping Spree

Subject: Friendship with mean girlz

Setting options: A local mall

Materials you'll need at your destination:

- $10 to $20 for the shopping spree
- This book

We're going to give your daughter the tools she needs to resist being a mean girl or to respond well when she's the target. I think that the most powerful way to explore this is experientially. But I really don't think either of us wants to put our daughters into a room of mean girlz to see how she comes out! So, let's try the next best experiential option: people-watching.

I'm sending you to the mall on a busy day or evening. Make sure it's packed with shoppers. You're going to offer your daughter a shopping challenge. After she completes it, you'll simply buy a lemonade or milkshake, plant yourself on a bench, and people-watch while you do your Girl Gab!

SKG Radio:
7-9 Minutes

Play "Date #3: Love Is Patient" in the car on your way to the mall.

Every time I visit the mall, I seem to find myself near someone being mean. A few weeks ago it was the woman in front of me at the checkout register of a clothing store. She was berating the clerk for running

SKG Challenge:
30-45 Minutes

out of gift boxes. In her mind, it was her right to have one. I've seen teenagers verbally accosting their moms for not buying them enough. I've seen friends yelling at each other down the hall. Sadly, I've even seen the moms be the mean girls. You might run into someone like this on your date. If so, I want you to take note of the experience to discuss it with your daughter.

To make this date fun, you're going to observe people while your daughter completes a fast-paced shopping spree. (This date has the *added* bonus of using the Secret Keeper Girl Truth or Bare Fashion Tests! Review these with your daughter before you shop. You can find them at secretkeepergirl.com or on page 69. Here's how it works:

- Give your daughter $10 to $20.

- Instruct her that she must purchase three things with her money, *each from a different store*. It works best if there is a theme to the shopping spree. For example, all three things must be fluffy or rainbow-colored or edible. If she has something unique going on, like redecorating her room or going on a special vacation, use that for a theme by saying, "Each item you buy must be for your newly decorated room," or "It has to be something you can take on our vacation." The point is to make it a little challenging.

- Tell her that she has only 30 minutes to complete her shopping spree or she forfeits what is left of the money. This will add an element of tension to the shopping, which will be good for the discussion you will have during Girl Gab.

- Finally, tell her to watch how other people interact with her and with others. Look for people who are having a hard time being nice for some reason. Observe their interactions for the Girl Gab time.

Ready? Set? Shop!

SKG Girl Gab:
15-25 Minutes

You'll use your Girl Gab time today to talk about Lucy the Leaver-Outer, Rule-Setting Ruth, Jealous Jane, and Beatrice the Queen Bee Bully. You'll learn about them in your Girl Gab section. Take a sneak peek so you can watch for them while you shop.

Your daughter's Girl Gab for this date is on page 165.

Hello, my Secret Keeper Girlfriend! How are you doing with your memorization? Me? I'm doing great. Hold on! Wait just one minute…

There!

I just recited 1 Corinthians 13:1-3 out loud.

Your turn. Say it out loud to your mom. Ask her to say it for you.

Keep working on it. Let's make it a goal to be able to say the whole chapter together. I totally promise that I'm memorizing right along with you.

Okay…on to verses 4-6.

> *"Love is patient and kind; love does not envy or boast;*
> *it is not arrogant or rude. It does not insist on its*
> *own way; it is not irritable or resentful; it does not*
> *rejoice at wrongdoing, but rejoices with the truth."*
> *1 Corinthians 13:4-6*

According to 1 Corinthians 13:4-6 and our SKG audio teaching today, fill in this blank.

True love is (patient).

Mean Girlz

Did you observe anyone being impatient at the mall today? Who?

(Daughter will write a description of who and what she saw today, if anything at all.)

What do you think they did wrong?

(Answers will vary.)

That brings us to an important subject, doesn't it? Sometimes people are really mean. Mean girlz come in all shapes and sizes and test our patience to the max. Here are a few:

Lucy the Leaver-Outer. The leaver-outer is not totally mean to your face, but she makes sure you aren't included in things. She might plan a party and not invite you or someone else in your group of friends. Occasionally, she's not that subtle. Take, for example, when she says: *"This seat is taken!"*

Rule-Setting Ruth. The rule-setter decides who is in and who is out. You never really know who will be her target.

Take this example:

Rule-Setting Ruth: "Hey everyone, we're going to pack our lunch in our Vera Bradley lunch bags tomorrow."

Ruth's target: "But I don't have one."

Rule-Setting Ruth: "Well, everyone else does, so let's do it anyway!"

Jealous Jane. Jealousy creeps in when you or another friend in the group achieves something special. Maybe you got your first A-plus. Jealous Jane often tries to "one-up" you by saying something like,

"Oh, I got an A-plus on the last test...and the one before that too. I would have had an A-plus on this test, but I helped my aunt move last night and I never got to study, so I only got an A-minus!"

Beatrice the Queen Bee Bully. Beatrice is the meanest of them all and might not be close to you. Most people are afraid that if they get too close to her, they'll be her target. So everyone lets her do her nasty stuff and just tries to steer clear of her cruel remarks like:

"Hey, Banana Bottom! Think you could have a bigger bottom? I could probably pop it with a pin!"

Okay, look back over those four mean-girl options. First, let me ask you to be over-the-top honest. Are you ever one of these girls? If so, put a square around that name. Take a moment to write a prayer of confession to God right here and ask him to help you to control your actions to be more like 1 Corinthians 13:4-6.

Now, go back to the list and use a circle to note any types of mean girlz you have to face at school, at church, or in your neighborhood.

How will you respond to that girl or those girls? Well, 1 Corinthians 13:4-6 gives you lots of ideas. Read over it and then rewrite a few ideas of how to respond here.

. . . .

. . . .

. . . .

. . . .

I want to focus on just one word of wisdom from 1 Corinthians 13. Go back and circle the words "Love is patient." I talked about these three words during your SKG Radio time today. What did I say that the writer of this book of the Bible, Paul, was really saying?

(He was saying that we should be "slow to boil.")

What does it mean to you to be "slow to boil" in friendships?

(Answers will vary but may include things such as "I don't get angry easily" or "I might be in a hot spot with a friend for a long, long time before I overreact" or "I need to learn to wait for God to work things out rather than getting angry!")

Today as you were shopping, you might have begun to feel what "boiling" inside feels like if you started to run out of time. Can you describe it?

(Answers will vary, but may include "you start to feel pressure inside"; "your body becomes tense"; "you feel like your heart might jump out of your chest.")

If you'd had all day to spend your money, you wouldn't have felt the same pressure and sense of "boiling." I think that sometimes the reason people are mean is because pressure is building up and too much is expected in a relationship. It's important not to put your friendships under too much pressure. Circle some examples of how *you* might put friendships under pressure.

- Demanding that your friend spend more or at least as much time with you as with anyone else.
- Asking a friend to not talk to certain people you don't like.
- Telling friends to dress or act a certain way.
- Always wanting them at your house.
- Always wanting to be at their house.
- Telling their secrets to other friends.
- Getting them in trouble at school or at home.
- Joining in when other people make fun of them or laugh.
- Nagging them to call you or e-mail you.
- Not including them in conversations.
- Talking about them to someone who doesn't like them.
- Ignoring them when you don't feel like talking.

Now underline any of those things that girls do to you.

Okay. Our goal is to be "slow to boil." To do that, we need to take off some pressure. Can you write one thing you need to do to take some pressure off of friendships where mean-girl tendencies might be creeping in?

(Mom's example: I feel frustrated when one of my friends doesn't call me for a few days. I know that's silly, but I think instead of expecting her to call me I will plan to start picking up the phone to call her when I feel that way.)

(Daughter's example: My friend likes to have a lot of friends. I need to start to realize that just because she is friends with someone else doesn't mean she's not friends with me. I'm going to stop complaining when she spends time with other people.)

Okay, practice that one thing until our next date and see if it doesn't make both you and your friend "slow to boil"!

SKG Radio:
3-4 Minutes

Pop in your SKG audio lesson to learn about how Christian recording artists BarlowGirl have dealt with mean girlz in their lives.

Pray for the mean girlz in your life. Ask God to give you patience for them and to help you to be "slow to boil."

SKG Driveway Prayer:
3-5 Minutes

Truth or Bare Fashion Tests!

Before we set you loose to shop, I have a few modesty tests every single outfit has to pass. I like to call them the SKG Truth or Bare Fashion Tests. If you did the Secret Keeper Girl dates on true beauty, cool fashion, and modesty, you already know them. Review each of the tests and take them as a group.

Test: Raise & Praise

Target question: Am I showing too much belly?

Action: Stand straight up, pretend you're really going for it in worship, and extend your arms in the air for God. Is this exposing a lot of belly? If it is, you may want to find a solution.

Solution: Go to the guys' department and buy a simple ribbed T-shirt or A-line tank top to wear under your funky short shirts, crop tops, or with your trendy low-rider jeans. Layers are a great solution to belly shirts!

Test: Grandpa's Mirror

Target question: How short is too short?

Action: Get in front of a full-length mirror. If you are in shorts, sit cross-legged. If you are in a skirt, sit in a chair with your legs crossed all ladylike.

Now, what do you see in that mirror? Okay, pretend that mirror is your grandpa! If you can see undies or lots of thigh, your shorts or skirt is probably too short.

Solution: Buy longer shorts and skirts!

Test: I See London, I See France

Target question: Can you see my underpants?

Action: Bend over and touch your knees. Have a friend or your mom look right at your bottom. Can she see your underpants or the seams in them? How about the color of them? Can she see your actual underwear because your pants are so low? If so, we have a problem!

Solution: Wear white panties with white clothes. If your pants are so tight that you can see the outline of your panties, try buying one size larger. If your pants are too low, throw on one of those guys' tank tops (we call them secret weapons!).

Test: Spring Valley

Target question: Is my shirt too tight?

Action: Before I tell you how to take this test, I should let you know that you might not need it just yet! It all depends on whether God has chosen for you to begin to grow breasts or not. (And his timing is different for all of us, so be patient!) Maybe you can have your mom take this test! Ask her to place the tips of her fingers together and press into her shirt right in the "valley" between the breasts. Count to three and have her take her fingers away. If her shirt springs back like a mini-trampoline, it's too tight!

Solution: Don't buy clothes based on size. Buy them based on fit. Often you have to go a few sizes larger these days to have a modest fit.

Test: Over & Out

Target question: Is my shirt too low?

Action: Lean forward a little bit. Can you see too much chest skin or future cleavage? If so, your shirt is too low.

Solution: Today's fashions thrive on low-cut shirts. Layering them is usually your only and best remedy. Throw on a little crew-neck T-shirt underneath, and you have a great look!

Friendship with My BFF

Challenge activity:
Create a BFF scrapbook

Key verse: 1 Corinthians 13:7a

Key thought: Real love doesn't gossip.

Suggested challenge setting: A favorite place to hang out with your BFF

SKG Prep Talk

Do you know what these "words" mean?[7]

LOL

J/K

BRB

GR8*

Okay, now let's take it up a notch. These are words that a parent *must* know! If you don't know them, your daughter probably shouldn't be experiencing any forms of Internet communication, for her own safety. See how you do with these:

---

* Laugh Out Loud, Just Kidding, Be Right Back, Great.

143
P911
MOS
KPC*

Those are just some of the words that fall under the category of what is sometimes called "Teenspeak." This global language bypasses national borders and, often, parental understanding. It's used by two-thirds of teens worldwide who text or chat with a friend from another country.

It's sending all the notions of classical grammar out the door—along with any sense of reservation concerning what the writer might say. With no face to match to the correspondence and the confidence that a parent could not possibly decode the messages, boldness creeps in, creating a sense of no restraint.

Gossip, slander, and bullying have found a new venue—one that takes it to an all-time high. The language and cruelty that we knew in our middle-school and high-school years has found its way to fourth grade. And it comes not only from strangers, but also from best friends who get lost in careless conversation.

"My daughter's not likely to do that," you say.

But will it be done *to* her?

What steps have you taken to train her to respond?

Prep Talk with God

Since we're on the subject of gossip, it might be a good idea to search your own heart. Romans 2:21 encourages us that we ought not to teach what we have not lived. As you spend this date teaching your daughter to control her tongue, take time to make sure that yours is under God's control. If it hasn't been, let this be your new beginning.

---

* I Love You, Parent Alert, Mom Over Shoulder, Keeping Parents Clueless.

A Date with your BFF!

Subject: Friendship with my BFF

Setting options: A fun place to hang with my BFF

Materials you'll need at your destination:

- A collection of photos of your daughter and her friends!
- Either a page or two for adding to an existing scrapbook, or a mini-scrapbook
- Store-bought cutouts and stickers or construction paper to make your own
- Scissors, photo tape, rubber cement, and so on
- A creative imagination!
- This book

A lot of the gossiping and bullying that your daughter will face in the next few years could come from online. However, at the ages of eight to twelve, I hope your daughter's access to e-mail and Internet is somewhat limited. As much as I wanted to take you both online to explore an interactive communication process, I just couldn't get myself to do it. Hold off on that as long as you can. But for this date, we'll explore the subject of how we talk to and about each other, which will hopefully overflow into her media-usage habits.

Instead of going online, we're going to create the old version of Facebook...a scrapbook! Girls still find this fun, and it's a tangible tool they can use to embrace their friendships! Just collect the materials and be ready to scrapbook until your hearts are content.

Your daughter's BFF can also be on hand to help. Connect with her mom and set up a time for your date. If your daughter's BFF is doing the SKG dates, she'll have her own materials to create a scrapbook page. If not, you can choose either to have her help with your daughter's scrapbook or to provide materials for her to create her own.

Do this date in a fun place like maybe a pavilion at a local park or the corner of a coffee shop!

SKG Radio:
7-9 Minutes

Play "Date #4: Love Protects" from your SKG audio file on your way to the SKG Challenge.

Create a page for an existing scrapbook, featuring your daughter and her BFF. Enjoy this time by just opening up your daughter's heart to friendship and the gift of God that it

SKG Challenge:
30-45 Minutes

is. Here are some great ideas to make your page or pages fun:

- Include a handwritten note from your daughter's BFF.
- Make a handwritten border out of Bible verses on friendship.
- Go to a Secret Keeper Girl Tour event and use photos of that on this page. (Go to www.secretkeepergirl .com for a list of upcoming tour stops.)
- Include a Top-Ten Memories list on the page mentioning all the crazy things your daughter and her BFF can recall.

- Write a list of five fun things your daughter and her BFF want to do together in the next year. Save a spread of her scrapbook for each crazy thing, and fill up the pages as you do the activities.

- Include a list of favorites such as "favorite dessert to eat together" and "favorite television show to talk about."

- Wear Secret Keeper Girl T-shirts (purchased at a Secret Keeper Girl Tour stop) and take a photo while you are there to include in the scrapbook!

SKG Girl Gab:
15-25 Minutes

After your scrapbooking activity, get alone with your daughter and use these Girl Gab pages to build a defense against gossiping!

Your daughter's Girl Gab for this date is on page 175.

Welcome back, SKG!

Before we start talking about why we did this date, can I ask you to recite 1 Corinthians 13:1-6?

The memorization for this date is so easy! We're only going to add three little words.

"Love bears all things…"
1 Corinthians 13:7a

Some versions say it more simply: "Love protects." According to 1 Corinthians 13:7a and our SKG audio teaching today, fill in this blank.

Real love doesn't (gossip).

Gossip is what happens when you hear a juicy secret from a friend, who heard it from another friend, who may have heard it from someone else, who might have made it up! Simply put, gossip is talking about someone in ways that aren't kind or truthful.

Chances are gossip is floating around your school and neighborhood just like it floats around mine. It might even creep into your church if you're not careful. Sometimes it's relatively harmless.

"Hey, I heard Jenny's dad has more money than the Jonas Brothers!"

But sometimes it's very hurtful to someone or to a group of people.

"Psst! Did you notice that the girl who sits in the front row of art class smells bad? I heard she hasn't showered in a month!"

Gossip is cruel, but there sure is a lot of it out there! Let's talk about gossip.

Mom, finish the sentences below and then share them with your daughter:

The most hurtful thing that anyone has ever said about me was...

. . . .

. . . .

. . . .

. . . .

This made me feel...

. . . .

. . . .

. . . .

. . . .

If I heard someone spreading gossip or lies about my BFF, I would...

. . . .

. . . .

. . . .

. . . .

True love doesn't gossip. Remember from our teaching that I told you that the New Testament of the Bible is written in which language?

Hebrew   Swahili   **Greek**   Martian

It's so much clearer sometimes when we can just hear what God was trying to say to us in Greek, so remember with me what he was really saying when he told us that love protects.

The original Greek wording actually said, "Love covers in silence"! What a great picture for friendship this creates. The next time you hear something from your friend or about her, make sure you "cover" her "in silence"! Simply put, keep her secrets secret.

When your friend tells you something private, it is one of the highest compliments you can get. She is saying, "I trust you!" Do you really want to lose that?

No way!

Cover your friend in silence!

There's only one really big exception to the rule of covering your friends in silence: If your friend is in danger, you need to tell an adult. *But not your other friends!*

SKG Radio:
3-4 Minutes

Pop on your SKG audio lesson to learn how Christian recording artists Barlow-Girl have covered in silence the secrets of their friends.

SKG Driveway Prayer:
3-5 Minutes

Ask God to forgive you if you have gossiped about anyone. Know that he will!

Friendship with My Parents

Challenge activity:
A date with Dad and some even furrier creatures

Key verse: 1 Corinthians 13:7b

Key thought: True love trusts.

Suggested challenge setting: A farm, pet store, or a zoo

SKG Prep Talk

I was in seventh grade when it happened.

"Want one?" a friend I thought I could trust asked, pushing a cigarette my way.

The first thought that ran through my head was loud and strong.

My dad is going to kill me!

"Uh, naw..." I stuttered. "I've already tried that before and I didn't like it much."

To this day I have never had a cigarette. In the awkwardness of the moment I felt the intensity of peer pressure and played cool to get off the hook, but in a million years I wasn't about to touch that cigarette. And it had everything to do with my dad.

Dads are safety mechanisms—there's no doubt about it. Girls who are close to their dads are less likely to participate in many risky behaviors. They are less promiscuous, less likely to develop eating disorders, less likely to experiment with drugs or alcohol, and less likely to drop out of school. [8]

Let's take that big fact to the Lord today and ask him what to do with it in your daughter's life.

Prep Talk with God

Pray about your daughter's relationship with her dad, even if—no, *especially* if—it is a strained and distant relationship. If your daughter does not have a father figure in her life, ask the Lord who can become that man.

PlanninG Date #5

A Date with Dad!

Subject: True love trusts.

Setting options: A farm, a pet store, or a zoo

Materials you'll need at your destination:

- Four-legged creatures to love and cuddle with or, if you're really daring, to ride!

- Your daughter's dad or a father figure, if her dad is not actively involved in her life

- This book

Today is just about hanging out with your daughter and her favorite guy, who is hopefully still Dad. Arrange a time when you, your daughter, and your daughter's dad can head off to spend some time together.

If that's impossible, know that the Lord didn't bring this into your hands to create yet another memory that your life isn't picture-perfect. He is not rubbing salt into your wounds. Instead, he is attempting to heal them. This knowledge is vital for you to have if your daughter doesn't have a good relationship with her dad. You need to be able to compensate for the void with godly male influence. This is your chance! Ask the Lord who could be the right man on this date. It's worth noting that if the man you choose isn't your husband or a male relative, the discretion of your interaction with him will speak volumes to your daughter.

Prepare him ahead of time by explaining the SKG dates and let him know what you'll be doing on this date specifically. (Read on to find out!)

SKG Radio:
7-9 Minutes

Play "Date #5: Love Trusts" in the car on your way to the SKG Challenge.

SKG Challenge:
30-45 Minutes

Your SKG Challenge is to simply spend time together interacting with animals. Little girls usually love animals, and maybe your daughter has a favorite. Does she love horses? Surprise her with a trail ride at a local farm! Is she crazy about pandas? Take her to see the pandas in Washington DC or San

Diego if you're close enough. Are you sad to say she's fascinated by bugs? A visit to a local university's entomology department will do just fine. The point isn't necessarily animals. The point is to spend time together.

What's the point of that? Well, research proves that parents who *do* things with their kids—doesn't really matter what—raise kids who are less likely to experience symptoms of classic teenage rebellion. Spend time with her!

Since our topic is trust, I've prepared some questions for you to cut out and put into a box for a game I like to call "The Box of Questions." (If you've completed the Secret Keeper Girl dates on true beauty, cool fashion, and modesty, you've already played this game.) Just turn to pages 182-183 and cut the questions into strips. Then, find or make a really special box to put them in. Any kind of special box will do. You could wrap a little jewelry box in festive paper or purchase a ceramic box that can be a gift to your daughter at the end of the game. Just make it fun.

Note: Please read through all of the questions to make sure you are comfortable with them. If your daughter will be experiencing this date with a grandfather or another male figure in her life other than her dad, you may want to rewrite them, using mine as guidelines.

SKG Girl Gab:
15-25 Minutes

Your Girl Gab for this date is the box of questions, but your daughter has some room in her journal pages to write some special memories. Here's how the game works:

1. After you've spent time interacting with the animals, find a cozy spot, maybe grab some ice cream or sodas, and pull out your box of questions.

2. Take turns pulling questions from the box. The person who pulls it tells who it's for—Dad, Mom, or daughter—and reads it.

3. The person it's directed to needs to do what is asked of him or her. The questions are mostly recalling memories or sharing opinions, so you can't get them right or wrong!

Your daughter's Girl Gab for this date is on page 179.

Note to moms: Because some daughters don't have dads at all or have dads who aren't willing or able to participate, your daughter's Girl Gab pages don't really mention that this is a date with Dad. That way, if she's with her grandpa or big brother she can enjoy it just as much! It's your job to explain the important role of the man in her life who is taking time to love her on this date.

Welcome back, SKG!

You should have a very special guest on your SKG date today! Let's start our Girl…er, Girl *and* Guy Gab right. Recite 1 Corinthians 13:1-7a for your favorite guy!

We're going to add just a little bit more of verse 7 today. In fact, it's so short that we're going to include what you learned on the last date.

"Love bears all things, believes all things..."
1 Corinthians 13:7a

You can believe in something if it is true. When there is someone in your life you can always believe, it is easy to trust them. What this verse is really saying is that we can trust someone who loves us. According to 1 Corinthians 13:7a and our SKG audio teaching today, fill in this blank.

True love (trusts).

There's a very old song that kids used to learn. It goes like this:

Trust and obey,
For there's no other way
To be happy in Jesus,
But to trust and obey.

It's not going to make it to iTunes anytime soon, but it teaches us a good truth. Trusting really is obedience. It's like *trust* and *obedience* are married to each other. You can't trust someone without obeying them or favoring their opinion and advice. Ugh! That's so hard, isn't it?

This is one of the greatest and hardest ways to show true love. Jesus even said, "If you obey my commands, you will remain in my love" (John 15:10 GNT). We show our love to God through trust and obedience.

We trust and obey God by trusting and obeying those he's put in authority over us. He's given you parents and other adults in your life to guide you toward him. We're going to spend this date exploring trust by playing a fun game.

The Question Box

Your Girl Gab for this date was to play "The Box of Questions" game. Did you like it? What are some of your favorite memories from the game? Write a few here.

1.

2.

3.

4.

5.

SKG Radio:
3-4 Minutes

Pop in your SKG audio file to learn how my friends—the BarlowGirl sisters— related to their mom and dad.

SKG Driveway Prayer:
3-5 Minutes

Spend some time praying for God to make you and your daughter trust-worthy and to give her the courage to trust her parents.

The Box of Questions for Date #5:

Friendship with My Parents

Dad: "What makes you trust your daughter? What qualities in her do you see that make you feel she'll make good decisions when you are not around?"

Mom: "What makes you trust your husband? Tell your daughter why you feel that his wisdom and advice can be trusted."

Daughter: "How does it make you feel when your mom or dad trusts you to do something new that you've never done before? Maybe you can start by remembering the last time that happened. Maybe you got to ride your bike further than before or go on a trip without your family."

Dad: "It's really important that your daughter trusts you to guide her concerning boys. How do you want to see your daughter interacting with them at her age?"

Mom: "When you were young was there ever a time when you broke your parents' trust? If so, how did you earn it back?"

Daughter: "Other than your mom and dad, who is someone older and wiser in your life that you would trust—that is, you'd not only tell them your secrets, but you'd obey their advice—and why?"

Dad: "Which of your daughter's friends do you trust most to help her make good decisions in life, and why?"

Mom: "Who is your best friend or an accountability partner? Tell your daughter what it is like to have a friend who knows everything about you and whom you trust to keep your secrets! Tell her about a time when you 'obeyed' her advice."

Daughter: "Other than trustworthiness, what are some of the qualities of love that you see in your dad?" (We've learned about acts of kindness, being patient, and not gossiping. You might select one of these and tell your dad how you see him live that out in his life!)

Dad: "What does it feel like to trust and obey God? Tell your daughter about a time when this was difficult for you, but you learned that you can trust him. Explain to her that even when other people fail her—and all humans may—God can always be trusted."

Friendship with My Siblings

Challenge activity:
Ding-dong-ditch someone

Key verse: 1 Corinthians 13:7c

Key thought: True love hopes for the best in someone.

Suggested challenge setting: Your kitchen and the front door of someone you know won't mind

SKG Prep Talk

"You do it," said 11-year-old Robby, offering Lexi the honor of ding-dong-ditching their grammy and grampy! They'd just baked a batch of fresh peanut-butter cookies and written a note from "The Backdoor Bandits"! Now they were ready to drop the goods.

"No, you do it," countered seven-year-old Lexi, staring up into her big brother's face. "You're faster!"

With that, Robby stood a little taller in the dark, took the cookies from her hand, and slunk off into the night!

Since my kids were small, Bob and I have always intention-ally offered ways for them to connect and interact. We have just always had an innate sense that they needed to solve problems without us, receive affirmation from each other, and have their own space where we didn't direct their relationship. One of my favorite memories was The Backdoor Bandits! But there have been many more.

Turns out that we were on to something and didn't even know it. Siblings are a great predictor of future behavior. Little girls who watch teen sisters get pregnant run a higher risk of getting pregnant. [9] Little siblings with teen brothers or sisters who engage in alcohol use are more likely to follow suit. [10] Of course, the opposite can be true as well. Little girls who watch older siblings make wise choices have a better chance of making wise choices.

Whether your daughter is a big sister or a little one, let's take some time to connect her to take advantage of that opportunity!

Prep Talk with God

Ask the Lord to guide you to select a sibling to connect your daughter to for this date, if she has more than one. Ask God to help you guide all of your children into good mentoring relationships with one another.

Planning Date #6

Ding-Dong-Ditch Date!

Subject: Real love hopes.

Setting options: Your kitchen and the front or back door of someone you know won't mind. (Options for young children are included in a sidebar on pages 96-97.)

Materials you'll need at your destination:

- Ingredients to bake a batch of your favorite cookies!
- A piece of paper and some colorful markers
- A sibling!
- This book

For this date, I want you to intentionally put your daughter into a setting where she is either mentored by an older sibling or mentoring a younger one. I think it's something we need to do as parents. It doesn't just happen. We set the stage.

"She's An Only Child!"

This date is still really important for your daughter. She needs to know that there are people in her life she can look up to and that *she* is being looked up to. Select someone from your church to play the part of a "big sister." Some good ideas include her favorite babysitter or an older cousin. It's not too early to start mentoring relationships.

If you're already doing this, great! This date will just be another fantastic memory for you.

If you've never considered it, let this be a fantastic beginning. All you need to do ahead of time is...

1. *Select your sibling!* Coach the older sibling a little bit in how to invest in their younger sibling. This may be your SKG, if she is oldest. Talk to her about the topic "Love Hopes." Tell them that as an older sibling, she should hope for great things for her

little sibs. Godliness, good friends, salvation, good grades, and wise choices for their whole life long. Clue them in to the fun you'll be having.

2. *Shop for cookie ingredients!* You can use your own favorite recipe or the one I provide in the SKG Challenge section.

SKG Radio:
7-9 Minutes

Set out all the things you'll need to start the date—from mixing bowls to the paper and marker to make a mysterious note for the cookies—on your kitchen counter. Bring the siblings into the kitchen and simply say, "I have a special challenge for you. You'll learn about it on this recording. I'll be nearby, but the success of this plan lies totally in your hands. Are you ready? Go!" Push "play" and listen to "Date #6: Love Hopes." Stay nearby and help as needed. (If your SKG is only eight and she's the big sister, you'll need to help a lot! But if your SKG has a big sister or brother on the scene, she's in good hands!) Do your best to give them room to solve their own problems and complete this challenge on their own.

Your SKG challenge—if you choose to accept it—is to "ding-dong-ditch" a favorite family with fresh, hot cookies. Here's one of my family's favorite recipes—Monster Cookies. I don't

SKG Challenge:
30-45 Minutes

make these often because they make a huge batch and last forever, but they are delicious—and the name is so appropriate as you send your cookie monsters off to do a secret mission.

Monster Cookies!

These cookies are ginormous (did you know that word is now in the dictionary?). You actually use an ice-cream scoop to put them on the cookie pan!

Ingredients

6 eggs
½ pound butter
1 pound brown sugar
2 C. white sugar
1/8 C. vanilla
½ t. salt

1½ pounds crunchy
   peanut butter
4 t. baking soda
9 C. rolled oats
½ pound chocolate chips
½ pound M&Ms

Instructions

Blend sugar and butter. Add eggs and beat. Stir in remaining ingredients. Drop with ice-cream scoop onto ungreased cookie sheets. Bake at 350 degrees for 20 minutes.

After your daughter and her cohort in crime have the first batch of cookies in the oven, give them the paper and markers to make a sign to leave their mark. It's so much more fun if you keep it a mystery! Suggest that they sign their note mysteriously with a name like "The Cookie Monsters" or "The Backyard Bandits"!

Once the cookies have cooled and are nicely packaged, send your children off into the night for the adrenaline rush of ding-dong-ditching! If you want, you can tag along with a camera to document the gang in action!

SKG Girl Gab:
15-25 Minutes

After the bandits are back where they belong, take some time to pull out your daughter's SKG Girl Gab pages for some heart-to-heart talk. You may consider photocopying the pages in her journal so that both of the siblings have a copy. Depending on the age of the sibling, you may need to modify the discussion questions.

Your daughter's Girl Gab for this date is on page 185.

Dates for Really Little Siblings!

Here are some other great ideas for how to approach "Love Hopes" if the siblings in your house are going to make a mess with a bowl of cookie dough.

Create a dress-up box
For a date with a toddler or preschool female sibling

Little girls love to dress up and they love their big sisters. (But they aren't great at holding meaningful conversations, so let's be creative in how we teach your SKG to be a great big sister!) During the challenge portion of the date, decorate a hatbox with construction paper, glitter, and paint with the name of the lil' sib. Fill the box with some of big sister's old stuff like an old dance uniform, a feather boa, worn-out ballet slippers, a favorite hat, and so on. After you've taken time to do the Girl Gab, invite your SKG to present the treasure to her little sister and to help her dress up.

Hello, my friend! I hope you just had a really special time with a brother, sister, or mentor in your life. Did you?

Let's start our Girl Gab time by reciting your memory verse for them. Recite out loud 1 Corinthians 13:1-7b!

Go bug hunting

For a date with a toddler or preschool male sibling

Little boys love adventures. (But they're probably not going to be good conversationalists for a *very* long time!) During the challenge portion of the date, decorate an empty plastic container with Sharpies. Be sure to include the name of the lil' sib between all those stars, hearts, and rainbows! After you've taken time to do the Girl Gab, invite your SKG to present the jar to her little brother and head outside to find some critters.

Write a letter

For a date with a brand-new baby sister or brother

If there's a new baby in the house, you and your daughter could probably both use a night off to get some time alone. Get Dad to give you a couple of hours at home alone to bake cookies and ding-dong-ditch someone...just the two of you. During the night, you'll take time to explain what an important job it is to be a big sister. At the end of the date, invite your SKG to write a letter to her new brother or sister about what she "hopes" for him or her. Put the letter in the baby's Bible for the future.

Now let's add the rest of verse 7.

> *"Love bears all things, believes all things,*
> *hopes all things, endures all things."*
> 1 Corinthians 13:7

According to 1 Corinthians 13:7 and our SKG teaching today, fill in this blank.

True love (hopes).

What do you think it means to hope? Write your answer below.

. . . .

. . . .

. . . .

. . . .

The dictionary says that hope is "the feeling that what is wanted can be had"! It means that you believe good things are going to happen in the future. It doesn't mean you believe that everything is just perfect right now.

Do you ever find that your sibling barges into your space without knocking? Or maybe he or she deliberately tries to annoy you with stupid jokes. That's sort of how it works with brothers and sisters, but under all of that there should be "true love," which includes hope for each other.

Hold that thought!

Let's take a quick test to see how well you know your sibling. Circle choices on both sides—one side for you and one for your sibling.

Mom, you should photocopy this or let your SKG's sibling use your book to fill this out. And you should take the test yourself for each of your children. Let's see how you do!

Which Do You Like Better?

You	Me
PB and J or grilled cheese	PB and J or grilled cheese
Dogs or cats	Dogs or cats
Sports events or musicals	Sports events or musicals
A beach vacation or camping in the woods	A beach vacation or camping in the woods
Pants or skirts	Pants or skirts
Board games or movies	Board games or movies
Winter or summer	Winter or summer
Pancakes or scrambled eggs	Pancakes or scrambled eggs
Snickerdoodles or chocolate chip cookies	Snickerdoodles or chocolate chip cookies
Math or English	Math or English

Okay, now compare! How well do you and your sibling actually know each other? If you did really well, congratulations! You must be spending some time together getting to know each other. Good job.

If you didn't know how to answer these questions at all, you are either 1) not spending enough time together or 2) in serious relationship trouble!

Does it matter if we know each other's favorites? Sure it does. It shows how much we take time to get outside of our own selfish desires to be concerned about our brother or sister. Do you know what he or she hopes to be when they grow up? Do you know how well your sibling is doing in school and what hopes he or she has to improve or stay on course?

When we know someone, it creates the knowledge we need to have hope for them.

What are three things that you hope for your brother or sister? Maybe you are still praying for your sibling's salvation. Perhaps you hope he or she can be a teacher someday because that's what he or she wants. Write three things below.

1.

2.

3.

Share your list with your sibling and let him or her share with you his or her hope for you.

An SKG Extra

Log on to www.secretkeepergirl.com to see how my daughters, Lexi and Autumn, got to know each other! It wasn't easy! They did not speak the same language...literally. Lexi speaks English and, at the time, Autumn only spoke Mandarin. (We adopted Autumn when both of the girls were 13, and they met for the first time in Nanchang, China!) But God has overcome every obstacle for them to "hope" the best for each other. Check out these fun videos for more details.

SKG Radio:
7-9 Minutes

Pop your SKG audio recording in to learn about how the BarlowGirls have "hope" for each other.

Guide your children in praying for one another. Pray over the list they wrote in their journal pages.

SKG Driveway Prayer:
3-5 Minutes

Friendship with God

Challenge activity:
A quiet encounter with God

Key verses: 1 Corinthians 13:8-11

Key thought: God is our only source of unfailing love.

Suggested challenge setting: Any place of solitude, such as a forest, a snowy mountain, the ocean, or even a candlelit bubble bath

SKG Prep Talk

Women really have a hard time finding the right place to plug into—and I'm not talking about how to set up your iPad, Wii, Blu-Ray player, or sound system! I'm talking about love!

We'll try just about anything to get love. Girlfriends. Careers. Volunteerism. Spiritual leaders. But I find that most of us spend far too much of our lives trying to plug into men.

In first grade I plugged into a boy named Gibby when he scrawled these words to me on a note: "I love you. Do you love me? Circle yes or no." (My mom still has the note.) I plugged into a boy named Sandy in seventh grade, who signed the back of his school picture, "To Dannah, who I met in seventh grade. The rest is history." What drama! Should I go on?

It takes us most of our lives to learn the fact that there's only one source into which we can plug and find unfailing love: God. Beth Moore points out that the Word of God uses the phrase "unfailing love" repeatedly, and there is never a reference to any other source than God himself. [11] Have you mastered that truth yet?

Start the lessons early and make the learning curve short for your little girl.

Prep Talk with God

Take a moment to ask God to help you to rely on him as your one and only source of unfailing love.

Planning Date #7

An Encounter with God!

Subject: Friendship with God

Setting options: Any place of solitude, such as a forest, a snowy mountain, the ocean, or even a candlelit bubble bath

Materials you'll need at your destination:

- Depends on the location you select
- A cell phone with a charger that does not fit it
- This book

Select your site. If weather permits, do this date outside. I always feel so connected to God when I'm not separated from his creation by man-made objects like walls and roofs!

After you've selected your site, determine if you will need any extra time for this date and collect any items you may need.

SKG Radio:
7-9 Minutes

Play "Date #7: Love Never Fails" on the way to your date location.

SKG Girl Gab:
15-25 Minutes

This date is unique. Your challenge is actually having quiet time with God, but you'll need to help your daughter get set up for this. So, we'll have our Girl Gab time first.

Before you open your journal, grab that cell phone and the charger that doesn't match it. (If you don't have two cell phones with different chargers, just about anything electric will work for this object lesson. A three-pronged electrical cord and a two-pronged electrical jack will suffice. Or you could use an international adapter and any US appliance. Be creative!) If you can, plug it in—your cell phone may read something like mine does when I try to plug it into Bob's charger: "Charger Rejected." Have this unique conversation with your daughter.

Your daughter's Girl Gab for this date is on page 189.

Here's a suggested conversation to get you started.

Mom: I want to show you what happens when I try to plug my cell phone into Daddy's charger. (Plug it in and let her read the message. Or you may let her see for herself that the plug won't even fit if you can't get it plugged in. As a last resort, you'll notice that the cell phone doesn't read "Charging" when the incorrect plug is used.) What's happening?

Daughter: (May say something about how the charger doesn't fit the phone.)

Mom: Will this charger ever work on this phone?

Daughter: (Will probably discern that it will not.)

Mom: Why?

Daughter: (That charger wasn't made to work with that phone.)

Mom: That's right. It's the same way in our lives too. Sometimes we try to plug into things emotionally that are not created to charge us up to love. That's what we're going to talk about today during Girl Gab. (Grab your journal pages and begin.)

Date #7: Friendship with God

Girl Gab

Where does real love come from? It's really easy to be emotional and girly and think that it comes from Prince Charming. We tend to believe that from a very young age. You could go your whole life kissing lots of frogs with that mentality and never really find true love. No, love doesn't come from some sort of romantic relationship. Today we'll explore the source of true love.

But first...how's that memorization coming?

Recite 1 Corinthians 13:1-7 out loud.

Keep working on it. Today we are going to add a huge chunk! You can do it. You've had it very, very easy for the last few dates.

"Love never ends. As for prophecies, they will pass away;
as for tongues, they will cease; as for knowledge,
it will pass away. For we know in part and we prophesy
in part, but when the perfect comes, the partial will pass
away. When I was a child, I spoke like a child,
I thought like a child, I reasoned like a child.
When I became a man, I gave up childish ways."
1 Corinthians 13:8-11

According to 1 Corinthians 13:8-11 and our SKG audio teaching today, fill in this blank.

Real love (never ends).

One version of the Bible says it this way: "Love never fails." I bet your friends have failed you. Some may have even stopped loving you altogether. I bet your teachers have disappointed you at times. Humans are imperfect and they will fail. Can you recall a time when you felt like someone who was supposed to love you disappointed you? Write about it below.

. . . .

. . . .

. . . .

. . . .

That hurt, didn't it? Of course it did! You know why? Read the verse below:

"What is desired in a man is steadfast love,
and a poor man is better than a liar."
Proverbs 19:22

The word "steadfast" means "unfailing." God created us to desire unfailing love. We are lying if we don't admit it. It's never wrong to feel hurt when we don't feel loved. It's a natural response, but if you spend all of your life trying to focus on love from humans, you're bound to feel hurt a whole lot. So, let's see if we can get you started in a better direction.

It's like when your mom tried to plug in two things that didn't belong together. What happened?

(Answers will vary: May include things like "they didn't fit" or "there was no power" or "trying to plug them in didn't make them work.")

There was no power in it.

Well, there's only one source of unfailing love and you've got to plug into it every day, my Secret Keeper Girl. Read the verses below and circle the only source of true, unfailing love, or stead-fast love.

> *"Let me hear in the morning of your steadfast love,*
> *for in you I trust. Make me know the way I should go,*
> *for to you I lift up my soul. Deliver me...O Lord!*
> *I have fled to you for refuge!"*
> *Psalm 143:8-9*

> *"I have trusted in your steadfast love;*
> *my heart shall rejoice in your salvation.*
> *I will sing to the Lord."*
> *Psalm 13:5-6a*

> *"We have thought on your steadfast love,*
> *O God, in the midst of your temple."*
> *Psalm 48:9*

There is only one source of unfailing or steadfast love, and it is God. You've got to "plug in" to him every day. Can you think of some ways that you can "plug in" to God? Write them below.

*(Answers can include "having devotions"; "reading the Bible";
"praying"; "talking about God to my friends and family";
"going to church"; and so on.)*

. . . .

. . . .

. . . .

. . . .

One of the best ways to "plug in" to God is to spend time with him every day. I want to challenge you to spend time with him regularly for the next two weeks. Will you sign my True Love Contract to make a commitment to do that?

The True Love Contract

Here's how it works.

1. Challenge yourself to spend time "plugging in" to God every day. I want you to do this for the next two weeks, for five out of seven days a week. (I'm giving you some days off!) To make it fun, put something on the line. For example, if you miss more than two days in a week, you might promise your mom that you'll organize her underwear drawer. (Ew! Yuck!) She might agree to walk the dog for you if she misses. It'll be fun to check up on each other. Keep it fun and light!

2. Agree to the challenge by signing the True Love Contract on the next page. When you get home you can tape it to your mirror or somewhere in your bedroom where you can see it every day.

TLC
True Love Contract

"Let me hear in the morning of your steadfast love,
for in you I trust. Make me know the way I should go,
for to you I lift up my soul. Deliver me…O Lord!
I have fled to you for refuge!"
Psalm 143:8-9

❀❀❀

Did I Spend Time "Plugging In" to God Today?

I, _____, will attempt to spend time "plugging in" to God through quiet prayer and Bible reading during the next two weeks. I will commit to doing this for five out of every seven days. If I miss more than two days a week, I will

. . . .

. . . .

. . . .

. . . .

for my daughter.

Signed: _____

Dated: _____

To make it easy, this book includes ten mini-devotions (see page 129) written by me and my Bod Squad—Suzy, Janet, and Chizzy. (They also helped me write a great fiction series that you should check out! Go to www.secretkeepergirl.com.)

Why not try one of the devos out right now?

SKG Challenge:
15-20 Minutes

After you've completed the Girl Gab, it's time to actually spend some time with God. Give each other a little space in the place of solitude you've discovered. Invite your daughter to turn to the first devotion on page 130. You'll read a scripture, then a devotion, and will end by writing a prayer back to God. If you want to do them separately, you may photocopy this section. Encourage your daughter each day in some special, positive way, like leaving a note on her door or offering to bake some warm cookies for her to munch on while she does her devos! Build this discipline in her now and it'll stay her whole life long!

SKG Radio:
3-4 Minutes

Pop your SKG recording in to learn about how BarlowGirl prioritizes "plugging in" to God as a daily practice.

SKG Driveway Prayer:
3-5 Minutes

As you arrive home, pray for the Lord to help you to keep your commitment of "plugging in" to him regularly for the next two weeks.

Here are some ideas about where you can go for this date. Be creative and consider your daughter's personality as you create this quiet encounter with the Lord.

Canoeing on a quiet lake

For our first SKG encounter with God, Lexi and I enjoyed an afternoon on a lake in a canoe. If you have a lake nearby, I would guess that there are some entrepreneurial spirits just as close by who would rent you a canoe. (Don't count on your daughter to help too much with the paddling!) Just Google "canoe rentals" with the name of your city and state and you should come up with some nearby options. Paddle up to a quiet bank for your time of solitude with the Lord.

Items needed: canoe, paddles, life vests (all supplied by a rental vendor), a blanket to sit on during Girl Gab, your daughter's favorite drink for a break.

A walk in the woods

I just love heading up to my parents' mountain house and walking through the untamed woods. I hold my breath in hopes of seeing a wild animal scurry by. To my delight I've seen dozens of deer, a mama porcupine with her babies, wild turkeys, and even one black bear! Find a place near your house where you can do the same. You can plop down on a blanket in the middle of the woods for your Girl Gab time.

Items needed: walking shoes, backpack for your books and drinks, a blanket to sit on for Girl Gab.

Snorkeling underwater adventure

This is for my friends on the coasts! I feel so connected to God when I see his underwater creation. Your daughter is just about the right age to give it a try for the first time. So, either head out to your local snorkeling rental store or...tuck SKG into your vacation luggage and take an afternoon for just you and your daughter. Of course, you'll have to find a dry place for your Girl Gab time, but it'll be a great start to your time with the Lord.

Items needed: snorkel masks, fins, life vests, swimsuits, towels, sunblock, and so on.

A sunset snack in a field

If the season is appropriate, find a beautiful field of wheat, sunflowers, or grass to nestle into while you watch the sun set. Enjoy your time with the Lord before the sun goes down, and then settle in to marvel at his miraculous handiwork as the sun sinks behind the earth.

Items needed: a thermos of hot chocolate or cool lemonade depending on the temperature, some finger foods, a blanket to rest on.

A bubble bath for one

Of course, it often happens that you can't get outside. Somehow you need to create atmosphere inside. One of my favorite ideas in the first set of SKG dates was to fill a bathtub with bubbles. Add a crystal bowl full of grapes and a goblet of grape juice and you have a delightful hiding place. Just shut the door and pray for your daughter while she soaks. Then, have your time together while she's wrapped up in her fuzzy robe!

Items needed: bubble bath, robe, grapes, and grape juice.

Friendship with Boyz

Challenge activity:
To play like the boyz

Key verses: 1 Corinthians 13:12-13

Key thought: True love pursues one lifelong relationship.

Suggested challenge setting: A laser-tag arena, a paintball field, or a go-kart track

SKG Prep Talk

I remember when *The Blue Lagoon* came out. My mom was up in arms about it. I was "never going to see that movie...ever." To this day, I haven't.

Many of my sixth-grade friends saw it that year. It made it all the worse for me, but it turns out that my mom was right.

A study on media, sex, and teens discovered that those who were subjected to heavy sexual media diets were 25 percent more likely to be sexually active.[12] Of course, these kids weren't viewing porn. They were just looking at the stuff the world throws at our kids on a daily basis as the norm. Early dating relationships, teen sex without consequences, and a constant diet of boy-craziness is marketed to our little girls through movies, television shows, and books.

You and I have to be countercultural if we're going to protect our little girls and teach them to approach guy-girl relationships in a holy and age-appropriate manner. What they have to face today is so much more aggressive than what you and I faced.

The Blue Lagoon was nothing.

Prep Talk with God

Ask the Lord to give you wisdom to help your daughter navigate the social pressure to be boy-crazy and expose herself daily to messages that feed that mentality. Pray that she would have an appetite for holiness. Remember, in the introduction to these dates I mentioned that being boy-crazy is an early indicator of a girl who might have many long-term boyfriends in high school, and that often leads to early sexual temptation. This is really important stuff, Mom. Equip her to wait!

Planning Date #8

Play like a Boy!

Subject: Friendship with boyz

Setting options: A paintball field, a laser-tag arena, or a go-kart track

Materials you'll need at your destination:

- This book
- Directions to a local paintball field, laser-tag arena, or go-kart track

- The same friends who attended your daughter's sleepover to kick off these dates (and their moms!)

Let's give your daughter some tools to resist being completely boy-crazy. I think the most powerful way to do this is to let her see that she's not alone. Other moms are asking their daughters to play it cool, and other girls are doing it. (My daughters are both 19, and neither had a boyfriend of any kind until they were seniors in high school. And those relationships were measured and appropriate. I'm so proud of them!)

In honor of the topic—boyz—we're going to do something boyz would love. (If your vocabulary doesn't include "Spyder Paintball Gun" or other brands such as Tippman, Ion, or Ultimate, this could be new territory for you!) You can select from a round of paintball or laser tag or a heated race in a go-kart. I'd go for the laser tag. It's a family favorite of ours! Every tiny ounce of testosterone that might be floating around me is absorbed into my system and I become completely competitive. I love it! (To see if there is a laser-tag arena near you, go to www.wheretoplaylasertag.com. For paintball or go-karts, check your local phone listings or search the net.)

After you've decided what you'll be doing, just schedule it and invite the same girls and their moms who joined you for the slumber party. (We're going to build positive peer pressure to resist boy-craziness. This is something that will be hard for your daughter to do alone, but with a great group of friends it is possible!)

It's a pretty easy date to plan!

SKG Radio:
7-9 Minutes

Play "Date #8: Friendship with Boyz" before you begin the SKG challenge.

Your challenge is to do something boyz love: paintballing, laser tag, or go-kart racing. Okay! Okay! Your girl might love these things already. I'm not trying to make a statement here. My girls love those things too.

SKG Challenge:
(Time depends on your selection.)

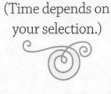

But they're a lot less girly than the other things we've been doing on our dates.

This is a great chance to just have fun with your daughter (and her friends and moms if you are doing this date as a small group)!

SKG Girl Gab:
15-25 Minutes

At your date location, find a private place to have a unique conversation about boyz. Explain to your daughter that there's one really important kind of true love that hasn't been discussed yet and today you're going to cover that.

I want you to begin by sharing with your daughter how very familiar your husband's (or best friend's) voice is to you. Share with your daughter how you can finish a sentence for him or can win a quick game of Pictionary because you have your own secret language!

If you are single, you can modify this section to skip the part about the dad. Again, I don't want this to wound your heart, and I urge you to confront any thought in you that might create such a wound right now. In Jesus' name, I want you to be strong and whole and confident that "he who began a good work in you [as a mom] will be faithful to complete it" no matter what your circumstances are.

It's so important for girls to know the beauty of marriage to be able to protect their future marriage! Your conversation could go something like this...

Mom: You know, a funny thing happens when I hear Daddy's voice. Before I even see him, I know it's his voice. I can be in a crowded room and when I hear my name, I know it's him. Do you have a relationship like that?

Daughter: (She may say that she recognizes your voice or a BFF's.)

Mom: I always recognize yours too. In fact, when you were little and we were on a crowded playground where dozens of kids were crying "MOM!" every few minutes, I never budged unless I heard your voice calling "MOM!" Then, I ran! I love hearing you call out my name—"Mom!" How does it feel when I call out your name?

Daughter: (She may not know how to respond to this one. It's pretty deep, but give her time to think and answer. She may say, "It feels good" or "It feels familiar.")

Mom: Back to Dad. You know, when I play a game with him, I can sometimes win just because I know him so well. Or when we are having a conversation, I often know what he is going to say before he says it. I *know* him, just like Dannah said on the recording. I love your dad so much. We aren't perfect, but we do love each other and that includes a "knowing"! We're going to learn more about that in your SKG journal today.

Your daughter's Girl Gab for this date is on page 197.

Date #8: Friendship with Boyz

Girl Gab

So, here we are in our final week. How's your memorization? Why not try saying what you have memorized so far?

Ready for our final verses?

*"Now we see in a mirror dimly,
but then face to face. Now I know in part;
then I shall know fully, even as I have been fully known.
So now faith, hope, and love abide, these three;
but the greatest of these is love."*
1 Corinthians 13:12-13

According to this verse and our SKG audio teaching, finish this sentence.

Love (knows) the one it loves.

Okay, crazy quiz time. Fast-forward with me to your wedding day. Here you are! Imagine with me…what is it like? What dress are you wearing? What kind of flowers are you carrying? Who is there with you? Maybe you've already dreamed about this day just a little bit. Can you dream on paper? Write two things about your wedding day that you hope for.

1.

2.

Secret Keeper Girl, our last Girl Gab is very, very deep. Buckle up! The ride may be bumpy. We're going to talk about boyz!

Read the two verses below and circle the word that is similar.

"Adam <u>knew</u> Eve."
Genesis 4:1a NKJV

"Be still, and <u>know</u> that I am God."
Psalm 46:10

❀❀❀

Both words—"knew" and "know"—actually mean "to know, to be known, to be deeply respected" in the original Bible language.

These verses are from the Old Testament—not the New, which is written in Greek. Any idea what language the Old Testament is written in? Give it a guess.

(Hebrew)

Anyway, back to our words: "knew" and "know." They're really talking about two precious and holy relationships. Which two relationships are mentioned in these verses? Circle two.

<u>**God and man**</u>

Brothers and sisters

Moms and daughters

<u>**Husbands and wives**</u>

That's right—the relationship between God and man *and* the relationship between husband and wife both get this special, holy word...to "know"! All through the Bible, God uses the same word to talk about his relationship with us *and* a husband's relationship with his wife. What does that tell you about a relationship between a husband and a wife?

(Answers will vary. She may say, "It must be pretty special."
She may say that it's like our relationship with God
in some way.)

If God wants you to get married someday, nothing will get in the way. But just like you and I are only supposed to worship one God, we need only one special relationship with a guy. The world may tell you that you need dozens and dozens of boyfriends by the time you are 16, but that's not God's desire for you. He wants you to have just one special man in your life, and it's not time just yet!

Do you feel any pressure to have a boyfriend or to be boy-crazy?

. . . .

. . . .

. . . .

If yes, what do you think causes that pressure?

(Answers will vary. She might say she feels it because all her friends are boy-crazy. She might say she just really likes boys. Whatever answer she gives, just listen. Don't correct or judge or try to change how she feels.)

. . . .

. . . .

. . . .

Now, back to our special verse in 1 Corinthians. It says, "Now I know in part." This sounds familiar. "Know"! What does the word "know" mean again?

(To know, to be known, to be deeply respected.)

In the New Testament, this word is used again to describe two relationships. Which two do you think? Write them below.

(Our relationship with God and our relationship with our future husbands.)

That's right! Our relationship with God. And our relationship with our future husbands. This earthly love of husband and wife is so special that it should be set apart to be pure and special. What can you do right now to set yourself apart from the boy-crazy world you live in?

(Answers will vary but may include "choose friends who are not boy-crazy"; "not watch movies and TV that make me boy-crazy"; "talk to Mom when I feel like I'm crushing on someone"; and so on.)

SKG Radio:
3-4 Minutes

Pop your SKG recording in to learn about how BarlowGirl approaches guy-girl relationships.

Pray for any boyz in your life who are friends. Ask God to help you approach your relationships with them in a way that honors him.

SKG Driveway Prayer:
3-5 Minutes

Part 3

Devotions and Other Good Stuff

Secret Keeper Girl Devotions

Secret Keeper Girl FAQs

Girl Gab Pullouts

Notes

Secret Keeper GIRL
Devotions

Okay, here we go into one of my most favorite parts of SKG... devotions! Each day during your SKG devotions, just read the scripture and the devotion of the day. Then, it's your turn—you get to write a prayer to God! This is everything you need to have some fantastic mother-daughter time together. Keep this book close and jump right into your time together by taking turns reading aloud!

Oh, by the way. I asked three of my close friends (*my* Bod Squad)—Suzy, Janet, and Chizzy—to write some of these. They also helped me write a crazy SKG fiction series about some girls named Toni, Kate, Yuzi, and Danika. (Check it out at www.secretkeep ergirl.com.)

Week 1

Week One / Day One
by Janet Mylin

Friend or King?
Read John 15:12-15

*"I look up at your macro-skies, dark and enormous,
your handmade sky-jewelry,
Moon and stars mounted in their settings.
Then I look at my micro-self and wonder,
Why do you bother with us?
Why take a second look our way?"*

PSALM 8:3-4 MSG

I hear so many worship songs that talk about God as our friend. One of my favorites says, "I am a friend of God!" These songs should always remind you that *God likes you*.

He *is* your Friend and even makes it a point to tell you so in John 15.

But, he's not just like any friend. My dad once told me something like this: "Be careful how you treat God. It's getting popular to call him your 'buddy' or 'pal,' but remember, he is God. He is King." When Dad said that, it made me realize that God is my dear, sweet, intimate friend, but I can't put him on the same level as my best girlfriends. He is also my majestic, all-knowing, supernatural King.

The friendship of God is like no other relationship. We need to enjoy him and laugh with him, but we need to worship him and honor him with all that we are.

In your journal today...

Make a list of how God is your Friend. Then make a list of how God is your King and Lord. Ask God to help you be friends with him while giving him great respect.

Week One / Day Two
by Suzy Weibel

The Beauty of God
Read Isaiah 53:2-6

"He had no form or majesty that we should look at him, and no beauty that we should desire him."

ISAIAH 53:2B

Where on earth do we get our ideas of what is beautiful? Six hundred years ago, wealthy girls plucked their hairline to make their foreheads seem higher. Ouch! Queen Elizabeth of England was thought to be beautiful because she was so pale. Many women used white lead on their skin to imitate her paleness, only to discover later that it was poisonous!

The Bible doesn't ignore beauty. It does, however, say over and over again that when we define beauty by what is on the outside, we make a *huge* mistake! A lot of people missed the glorious beauty of Jesus Christ because he had "no beauty that we should desire him" on the outside. Think about that! Jesus wasn't beautiful by the world's standards. And yet, there's no doubt you'll never have a better friend!

I wonder how many great friendships you and I have missed out on because we have gotten caught looking only for outside beauty?

In your journal today...

Rewrite Isaiah 53:2b in your journal. Then write Jesus a letter telling him all of the reasons that he is beautiful to you.

Week One / Day Three

by Chizzy Anderson

Do the Dance
Read Luke 15:11-25

"The LORD thy God in the midst of thee is mighty; he will save, he will rejoice over thee with joy; he will rest in his love, he will joy over thee with singing."

ZEPHANIAH 3:17 KJV

My mom did the craziest thing when I accomplished something great. She would hop-dance and clap while singing the King James Version of Zephaniah 3:17. I have a vivid picture of her doing this as if it were yesterday, even though it's been years. Watching her dance enthusiastically over something I'd done showed me a little of what God does for me. He dances over me. He sings his love out to me. The awesome and mighty God of the universe can sing and be ecstatically joyful over me? It blows my mind!

But God doesn't just dance over us when we do something great or worthy of praise. He dances over us just because we are near. As you read Luke 15 today, you may have noticed that the prodigal son wasn't off doing great things. He was rebelling. But when he came close, his dad danced like my mom. He danced just because his son came back.

God is like that. He dances over you when you do great things. He dances over you just because you get near to him. He dances over you because he's crazy about you and can't help himself. He's willing to go to extreme measures to express his joy over you.

In your journal today...

Today, put your journal down. Get a favorite song going on your iPod and dance right back at God! You're going to love it!

Week One / Day Four
by Janet Mylin
Are You a Fan?
Read 2 Samuel 6

"...I will make merry before the LORD. I will make myself yet more contemptible than this."

2 SAMUEL 6:21-22A

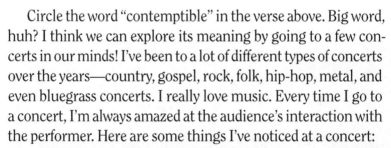

Circle the word "contemptible" in the verse above. Big word, huh? I think we can explore its meaning by going to a few concerts in our minds! I've been to a lot of different types of concerts over the years—country, gospel, rock, folk, hip-hop, metal, and even bluegrass concerts. I really love music. Every time I go to a concert, I'm always amazed at the audience's interaction with the performer. Here are some things I've noticed at a concert:

...the fans want to be as close to the celebrity as possible and will pay a ton of money to get those seats.

...the fans watch every single move the celebrity makes and hang on every word.

...the crowd is absolutely craving an opportunity to scream, clap, raise their hands, and yell, "We love you!"

...when the entertainer exits the stage, the crowd begs and yells for more and isn't satisfied until the band comes out and does one more song.

...true fans have absolutely no shame in expressing how much they love their favorite singer or band.

That's pretty much contemptible behavior. To be "contemptible" is to be unlikable or vile in behavior. The verse is saying that King David was shameless in expressing his love and devotion to the point of being unlikable to others. That's serious celebration!

When is the last time you felt no shame in worshipping God? Are you willing to give everything you have to get as close to him as possible? Are you desperately trying to get a clear view of every move he makes? Do you hang on God's every word by reading your Bible? Do you beg him for more insight into who he is?

In your journal today...

Think about how you would act if you were to meet your favorite celebrity. Compare this to how you think you would act if you met Jesus face-to-face. Write about this comparison and ask God to help you become one of his biggest fans!

Week One / Day Five
by Dannah Gresh

Turtle Shields

*"Take up the shield of faith,
with which you can extinguish all the
flaming darts of the evil one."*

Ephesians 6:16

In ancient Rome, each warrior was given a huge shield for battle. Each one was the size of a door. The cool thing about these shields is that they were like puzzle pieces and could lock into each other. That way, when the battle got intense, the soldiers could create a ginormous wall to hide behind. In the worst of battles, they made a circle with the shields on the outside and put a few above them. This created a sort of "turtle shell" to hide in when the enemy sent flaming arrows.

This is a picture of what true friendship can be. You and I are in a constant battle with the enemy of God, Satan. He's going to throw a lot of flaming arrows at us, like sadness, jealousy, broken friendships, sickness, and even big family problems. While you can't stop those arrows from coming your way, you can keep them from penetrating into the core of who you are. How? By having friends who will war with you in prayer. Consider every time you pray with friends that God is building a "turtle shell" around you with your "shields of faith." You cannot see it with your eyes, but it's ginormous and solid! Wow!

Of course, your friend only has a shield to lock into yours if they too consider God a dear friend. Are your girlfriends also friends with God? Why not begin, while you are young, to pray with your friends?

In your journal today...

Write a list of friends you can turn to when you need to pray because they are also prayer warriors. Then, write a word of thanks to God for these friends.

Week 2

Week Two / Day One
by Dannah Gresh

Long Live... You!
Read Exodus 20:1-21

"Children, obey your parents in the Lord, for this is right.
'Honor your father and mother'
(which is the first commandment with a promise),
'so that it may be well with you,
and that you may live long on the earth."

EPHESIANS 6:1-3 NASB

Once when I lived in an area just outside of Tornado Alley—
the part of the U.S. that gets struck with the most tornadoes—
a dark cloud settled over all of our city. Not a soul stirred in that
purplish, heavy haze. We were scared silly!

Maybe that's why I just go crazy when I read Exodus 20:21.
Did you read it? It says, "The people stood far off, while Moses
drew near to the thick darkness where God was." Picture it. Two
million or so scared-out-of-their-shorts Israelites gaze up at a
"thick darkness" or a massive, dark cloud. God is in that cloud.
It has to be scary, but Moses approaches it to be near to God!

I'd like to approach God with that kind of security and courage, wouldn't you? Well, Moses could because he was a man who
honored God's commandments. Let's look at one that's important to our relationships: "Honor your father and mother." Did
you know that God promises you'll live longer if you are obedient to your mom and dad? That sounds very possible. Children who don't obey their mom and dad often get into all sorts

of crazy situations as teenagers. Sometimes their bad decisions lead to sickness or addiction to things like alcohol. It's no way to live. And their lives are more at risk of being cut short.

Want to live a long life? Honor your mom and dad!

In your journal today...

Write a letter to God telling him what the best thing about your parents is and what is hardest. Ask him to help you to honor them even though there may be challenges.

Week Two / Day Two
by Chizzy Anderson
Obey the X-Ray
Read Genesis 19:12-29

"Do not be deceived:
'Bad company ruins good morals.'"

1 CORINTHIANS 15:33

"I would prefer that you didn't hang out with (insert friend's name here) anymore." My mom said that more times than I cared to hear it. You want to know the crazy part? Most of the time, my mom would say it *before* the "friend" had done anything wrong! But, if my mom said it, it was pretty certain something bad would go down!

It seems as if parents have this God-given ability to see through your friends and into their hearts. Kind of like some sort of character X-ray. They can usually tell when the good things you've learned are in danger of being misled by "bad company." That's what happened to Lot's wife in Genesis 19.

She made some of the most wicked people on earth—from Sodom and Gomorrah—her best friends. It didn't end well for her! If only her mom had been around to say, "You can't hang out with them!"

If you think you're hanging out with someone so you can rescue them, consider this: You may not be strong enough just yet. It will be like trying to save someone from being swept away by a raging river without first securing yourself. Somehow your parents know whether you're strong enough to yank your friend to safety or if you'll be swept away.

It's hard to obey your mom or dad when you don't see what the big deal is, but that's when it's even more important to trust the people in your life. Remember, God gave you this person with super-special X-ray vision to protect you.

In your journal today...

Have your parents ever asked you to spend less time with someone? How do you feel about separating yourself from them? Take a few minutes to pray for them and to ask God to help you obey your parents' X-ray vision.

Week Two / Day Three
by Janet Mylin
Control Freak
Read Genesis 4:1-12

"Wrath is cruel, anger is overwhelming,
but who can stand before jealousy?"

PROVERBS 27:4

Do you find that it's easy to be jealous of some of your friends? Or are you jealous of those girls at school that seem to have everything—the clothes, the personality, the hair, the boys? Everyone struggles with jealousy now and then. No one plans to get jealous. It just happens. You can't control that it happens, but you can control what you do with those nasty feelings.

If you don't choose to control jealousy, your story can turn out a lot like Cain and Abel's did in Genesis 4. You won't end up killing someone, but you might end a relationship or destroy someone's reputation with those emotions. When you're jealous of someone, it almost always turns into something really bad, unless you and God deal with it together.

The best remedy I've found for overcoming jealousy is to do everything I can to control my focus. Our focus shouldn't be on other people. It should be on God. As we learn more about him, we'll become truly thrilled with who he created us to be. You see, a lot of times jealousy is all about focusing on what we're *not*, rather than what we are! This is one area of your life where it pays to be a control freak!

So, just in doing this awesome SKG devo challenge, you're on the right track. You're focusing on God. Tomorrow, Suzy will give you more ideas about how to tackle jealousy. Until then, try this journal assignment.

In your journal today...

Who are you jealous of ? What are you jealous about? Write it down. Now write down something about yourself that God made pretty special. Write God a letter and ask him to help you overcome the jealousy.

Week Two / Day Four
by Suzy Weibel
My Friend Is a Superstar
Reread Genesis 4:1-12

"The eye cannot say to the hand, 'I have no need of you,'
nor again the head to the feet, 'I have no need of you.'"

1 CORINTHIANS 12:21

I have a friend who is truly a rock star! Her name is Stephanie Smith, and she's a Christian recording artist—but I knew her before all that! I've known her for over ten years, and I've always known she was going to be famous for her great voice. In fact, the first single she released was called "Superstar" and she really is one!

Do you have a friend who everyone says is going to be famous someday? Maybe she's an amazing singer or dancer. Or she plays the piano like a pro and is a great actress. Maybe she makes everyone laugh or dominates on the basketball court. Everyone likes her and wants to be around her. Here's the hard part: Sometimes being around people God has gifted so extraordinarily can make you feel invisible. How does a girl overcome that kind of jealousy? I have a good thought for you—your friend *needs* you!

Your friend is going to need the gifts that you have to offer—gifts that she doesn't have. She may not be good at running from temptation, at seeing when other people need prayer, at inviting people to be included, or at being obedient. Steph was asked to write a book to release with her first CD. Guess who got to help her write it? *Me!* What an honor! She needed me!

You have a special gift to give this friend, or God wouldn't have put you into her life. Ask him to reveal to you why your super-star friend needs you.

In your journal today...

Confess your insecurities to God. Then, with his help, write down all of the ways in which he has gifted *you* to be a super-secret-keeper-girl-star to your friend!

Week Two / Day Five
by Suzy Weibel

Slumber Party Gone Bad...
Read Daniel 3

"Our God whom we serve is able to deliver us from the burning fiery furnace, and he will deliver us out of your hand, O king. But if not, be it known to you, O king, that we will not serve your gods or worship the golden image that you have set up."

DANIEL 3:17-18

I was always one of those odd kids who actually preferred to sleep in my own bed—I did like to spend the night with friends, but I preferred the sleepover to be at my own house. Maybe there were a few selfish reasons. I liked my mom's food the best. We had a swimming pool. I didn't like to be away from my pets.

And at times the rules I was familiar with went out the door at other people's houses. I knew that sometimes my parents wouldn't approve of games we were playing or movies we were watching. I felt very awkward in these situations. I would wonder things like, "Should I call my mom? Should I say something to my friend's mom? Do I participate or sit out? Will I be made fun of if I don't go along with everyone else?"

When Shadrach, Meshach, and Abednego were faced with doing something wrong—when they were asked to worship a false god—they didn't have to make a decision alone. All three were in agreement that they would not do what the other people were doing, even if it meant getting burned. It is so hard to stand alone, but when you stand with a girlfriend on your right and one to your left, it's not such a hard thing after all. Do your friends help you stand for what is right?

In your journal today...

Write a letter to God in your journal asking him to make people notice that you refuse to be like everyone else. Tell him how you plan to stand (with friends) for all that is right!

A note from Dannah: I like to call my closest circle of friends my Bod Squad! They're the ones who help me stand tall. Pick out your Bod Squad and join us! Go to www.secretkeepergirl.com for a listing of upcoming event locations.

Secret Keeper Girl

FAQs

Hey, Secret Keeper Girl moms—

I know you still have lots of questions about your tween daughter, so I've included a few of the most commonly asked questions we receive on our Secret Keeper Girl website and blog. These seem to be the ones that most often race through moms' minds when they're thinking about friendship, boys, and mean girls.

I encourage you to dig deep into God's Word with your daughter to find the answers to all the questions you have, whether or not I mention them here. As you dig deeper into the Word together, know that it will reassure her that you do treasure both her and the life God has designed for her.

To get you started, here's a list of questions I discuss in this section:

- When should I let my daughter start dating?
- When should I let my daughter wear makeup?
- What should I do about cliques?
- When should I let my daughter start wearing a bra?
- Should I be "friends" with my daughter? How do I

find the balance between being her parent and still helping our relationship grow?

- Should I be concerned about "sexting" yet, or just when my daughter is older?
- How do I know if my child has been abused?

When should I let my daughter start dating?

I recently worked with a mom who was distraught that her son was "dating" a girl in middle school. I first asked her how old she'd hoped he'd be before he dated and she said, "Sixteen." Then, I asked her when she'd ever talked to her son about that. She just looked at me, puzzled.

"Well, he's only in seventh grade," she said. "It wasn't time to talk about it yet."

"Obviously it was," I said.

By the time a girl is 11, 30 percent of her peers will have had a boyfriend. [13]

At some point, you have to tell your kids point-blank about what your standards are. We adopted our dating protocol after reading a book. We decided to let our teenagers go on group dates for special events as soon as they hit high school. That means they could go on a chaperoned formal event, if they wanted, at the age of 14 or 15. Rob took advantage of this. Lexi did not. The first boy asked her by writing it on a piece of paper and whacking her in the head with it. The second one had already asked her friends. So, she decided to dress to the nines with five other girls and take public transportation to her first formal.

Our teenagers were allowed to go on single dates when they were 16, as long as we were actively involved in the planning and execution of the evening. What do I mean by "actively involved"? Well, Lexi and Autumn always knew that a guy who wanted to take them out has to go through an interview with their dad. Period. If the boy seemed to have honorable intentions and was someone we felt comfortable with, we most likely allowed them to spend a carefully planned, very public evening together. We were approving everything they did, and they were in close contact with us. That's what I mean by involved.

Finally, we discouraged them from being in any exclusive relationships until they were out of high school. We really wanted them to enjoy high school free from the drama that relationships can bring, and we didn't want their heart wounded by excessive relationships.

I can't overstate the importance of communicating these standards when your daughter is a tween, even if that seems difficult. I also can't understate how easy it is. My kids' hearts were so innocent that it was just comfortable and natural to discuss. It's easy to establish your standard if you do it before the hormones kick in and "everyone else" has a boyfriend. If you wait, you may find yourself working a lot harder.

When should I let my daughter wear makeup?

If your tween is begging you to wear makeup, listen to this before you give in: Researchers from the Medical Institute for Sexual Health found that one of the top five factors placing a girl at risk for sexual sin is appearing older than she actually is. Wearing makeup plays a big role. Emphasize to your tween daughter that makeup isn't necessary to enhance her beauty. Special lip gloss—and in some extreme cases, corrective base makeup—is okay and shows her you're not trying to take away her fun, but overall makeup can wait!

Instead, call attention to specific and unique beauty strengths of hers. For example, "Your eyes are showstoppers! They're so bright and blue I think I could swim in them!" or "You have very creamy, white skin. It reminds me of Snow White!"

What should I do about cliques?

Welcome to the years of *homophily*. That's a fancy psych term for cliques. While I don't like cliques, and we've worked hard to keep our kids from forming them, they're pretty much inevitable. And they can even do some good. Somewhere around the tween years, your daughter will start to select people who are like her to be her friends. Conversely, whoever she picks to be her friends will affect who she becomes. Friendships formed in the tween and teen years have significant influence on all types of behaviors. Like it or not, your daughter's friends will either support the values you are attempting to instill or overwhelm your daughter with a different point of view.

So what's a mom to do? Get involved in her friendships! My mom did this when I was growing up, and it was a critical maneuver in protecting her little girl (me!). Part of me wanted more space, but most of me loved that my mom was the mom everyone could really talk to. In fifth and sixth grade, my friends shared their drama with her as if she were a highly paid counselor. As a result, she was on the inside of our major decisions. It also gave her the knowledge to step in if I was making wrong decisions.

It can get tricky here since, as you've already learned, somewhere between the ages of eight and twelve, many girls tend to feel strongly that Mom should not be involved in friendships or help select them. This is no small issue to be tackled. The Bible tells us, "Whoever walks with the wise becomes wise, but the companion of fools will suffer harm" (Proverbs 13:20). It's critical for you to be involved in her friendships so you can teach her during these tween years how to select friends who will mirror her values and stand strong with her in her teen years. The goal is not complete control, but informed guidance.

I suggest you do this by becoming the ultimate Carpool Queen and Sleepover Diva! Driving carpool is a great way to do research on your kids. If you keep the volume on your radio turned down, you can really tune into the generally unfiltered interaction of friends. You learn who burps the loudest, who the meanest teacher is, and who has a boyfriend. Just enjoy and learn. God will guide you in how to use this…ah…"intelligence" later on.

You can also make your home *the* place to hang out. Become the hostess with the mostest. Make your home kid-friendly—whether that means a pool, a secret room, a basement with a big screen, or an old air-hockey table. Host game nights or movie nights and *earn* the status of hangout. Why? So you can protect your daughter! It's smart to be the host home. So pop the corn and pull out the sleeping bags that will never be used for sleeping. A connecting mom is a Sleepover Diva.

As an added bonus, being the host home lets you introduce your daughter to girls who may not naturally be part of her clique. Take advantage of the opportunity to reach out to that girl at school or church who always gets left out or maybe doesn't have an involved mom in her life. This is a great way to model compassion for your daughter, teaching her how to befriend those the rest of the world deems "unlovable."

When should I let my daughter start wearing a bra?

You've heard me say a lot about the importance of keeping your daughter from growing up too fast. It seems this is an issue directly related to that, so let's talk!

Maybe you remember when Abercrombie Kids, the children's division of Abercrombie & Fitch, marketed a padded push-up bikini top for girls as young as eight. (Most eight-year-olds don't even have anything to push up!) It was labeled the "Ashley" triangle top, and after widespread parental disapproval was taken down almost as soon as it was posted. I asked my Secret Keeper Girl moms to contact Abercrombie Kids and demand that the product be removed. Why? Because it was a direct assault on our daughters.

An American Psychological Association task force report links mature clothing marketed to younger and younger girls, the sexual content of the marketing, and the sexual overtones of the products themselves to eating disorders, low self-esteem, and depression when these girls become teenagers. Normalizing this kind of clothing only makes it a more and more difficult battle to dissuade them from wanting you to buy this stuff. We have to stick together to protect our daughters.

However, there will come a time when your daughter *will* need a bra! Your daughter is going to be curious at some point, and that in itself might be a sign that it's time to talk turkey. Generally around age ten (but sometimes as early as eight) your little girl will start to develop breast buds. Although a ten-year-old certainly doesn't need thick padding or a push-up bikini top, she may start to feel uncomfortable if those new "developments" can be seen through her shirt. In this case, look for a lightly-lined or lightly-padded product to do the trick.

Let me also suggest that wearing a bra isn't something that makes your daughter necessarily appear older (which is something that I've talked about a lot because it's dangerous for her)—but at a certain point, withholding it when it's something she desires may leave her open to being made fun of. If it's time to take her bra-shopping, then help her pick out some super-cute ones! And of course, finish off the trip with smoothies and girl talk—maybe even make it another great date!

Should I be "friends" with my daughter? How do I find the balance between being her parent and still helping our relationship grow?

That sure is a difficult balance, and a lot of parents never find it. As moms, we tend to fall into one ditch or the other. Either we try to be our daughter's best friend and ignore the precepts we're supposed to be writing on her heart, or we veer to the opposite side of the road and become a tyrant who helicopters over our daughter, preventing her from seeing that our precepts are set in love.

It *is* possible to avoid extremes and develop a strong, healthy relationship with your daughter while still acting as her parent. (But keep in mind that a strong, healthy relationship doesn't mean she'll always *like* you.) To find the balance, try not to focus so much on your relationship with your daughter. Instead, focus on the truths of God's Word. Remember that when you bring truth to somebody with all kinds of grace, it's loving. And conversely, when you bring truth with no grace at all, it's harsh.

During your daughter's tween years, your main job is to be her counselor. She's developing her own set of moral values by asking you *why* you believe what you believe and do what you do. In her little brain she's asking, "*Why* does Mommy do that? I think I want to be like Mom, but does it *really* feel good? Maybe I will do it too, if she can tell me why." She's beginning to monitor her own conduct based upon her own reasoning. Which means she'll ask a lot of questions. You get to be her counselor as she figures out everything she believes about life!

During those times when you're enforcing a rule she doesn't like, you can hug your girl and say, "I'm so sorry you don't like this truth, but you have to agree with me that it's truth, right? It stinks that we have to submit to this sometimes. But we have to. And this is the reason why."

Should I be concerned about "sexting" yet, or just when my daughter is older?

Well, frankly, I hope you'll wait a few years to give your daughter a cell phone. Waiting is good. It builds discipline. My daughters were 13 when they got theirs. I kind of wish I'd waited until they were 16, like I did with my son, Rob. You may have a good reason for your daughter to have one sooner.

Either way, sexting is a good thing for you to get on your radar. A few years back, I was devastated to find that two of my teen mentees were caught up in the nasty world of sexting. One of them, a sweet homeschooled Christian girl, actually sent a topless photo of herself to a guy. The other, a pastor's daughter, was graphically propositioned for sex through a text message that ended with "I know your dad is a pastor, but this is none of his business." As a mom, that should make your blood boil! It does mine.

If you have a teen, don't be naïve. The stats are alarming—45 percent of teens say they've sent or received a sexual text message. One in five admits to sending or receiving nude photos. This is *common*! (I loathe to use that word for something so vile.) Let me say it again—don't be naïve. My friend Vicki Courtney noted on her blog that 50 percent of parents whose teens *are* sexually active believe they are not!

How can you know if your teen or tween is involved in something they shouldn't be...particularly sexting? Talk to them! Ask them. Let them know of the dangers, including the fact that sending or receiving nude photos of someone who is under 16 is considered a crime of child pornography. There are stiff penalties for this, including jail time (though this is very unlikely for younger teens and tweens). Often just asking questions will help your child feel comfortable to open up with you about what they are feeling pressured to do. If they don't open up to you, or you become suspicious because of an odd reaction, just ask them to let you check the history on their cell phone. You can look together.

What happens if you find that your child is sexting? I'd be radically protective of them. Contact your cell-phone service provider and change their service to exclude the texting feature. If they themselves have been sending "sext" messages, let me suggest something very loving—*take away their phone*! Let them re-earn your trust and get the phone back when they have. Seem extreme? Consider this: How meaningful and helpful to good human communication is a text message? I mean, really! (I do know this: It's very bad for your child's grammar.) Instead, invite their friends over and encourage some good old-fashioned face-to-face friendship.

How do I know if my child has been abused?

Child sexual abuse. It's often on the hearts of the staff at Pure Freedom (the name of our overall ministry) because moms do contact us for advice on how to help a daughter or son through this nightmare. Sadly, our ministry receives a lot of these requests for boys and girls of all ages. Fact is, about 15 to 25 percent of adult women and 5 to 15 percent of adult men were sexually abused as children. It's a frightening reality.

How can you know if your child is a victim? Watch for these signs. First, watch for a sudden and unusual interest in sex or sexual things. Second, consider that sleeping problems or nightmares that seem to stem from nowhere could be a symptom. Third, an unusual fear of going to a certain house, school, or class is sometimes a sign that something bad has happened in that place. Fourth, children who are abused often attempt expressions of sexual molestation in artwork or in their actions during play. These things can be evidence that it's time for you to dig a little deeper to see if there's something your child desperately wants to tell you, but doesn't know how.

If you do find there's abuse present, act quickly to get your child into the care of a trained counselor who can help you and your family make good decisions about the best course of action. Each child, each situation, is different, but every child is tender and needs meticulous attention to specific needs.

Just for You, God's

Secret Keeper GIRL

Girl Gab Pullouts

True Friendship in God's Eyes

Welcome to SKG! That stands for Secret Keeper Girl, and I'm hoping you'll want to be one if you aren't already. If you did the 8 Great Dates on true beauty, cool fashion, and modesty, you know that a Secret Keeper Girl is *a masterpiece created by God*. That's the core of what and who you are! But... just how does a masterpiece created by God live and interact with all of God's other great masterpieces like your mom, dad, BFFs, and boyz? That's what we're going to discover during these eight great dates! Earlier I introduced an important quality that's in every SKG. Do you recall what that is?

A Secret Keeper Girl pursues _____.

"Pursue love."
1 Corinthians 14:1 NASB

Love Meter

Okay, let's take girl talk to a new level. It's called Girl Gab. So, are your friendships more like that game of sixes or more like that sweet SKG-Style Memory Pillow experience? Let's find out by taking this Love Meter test.

Read the following scenarios and decide where they'd rank on the Love Meter.

 Your friend meets someone new at camp, you decide it's not fair that she doesn't spend all her time with you, and you give her the silent treatment the rest of the week.

You see your friend out riding her bike with the new girl in the neighborhood. The next day on the bus, you ask her how you can encourage that girl too.

It's summer break and things in the neighborhood aren't going so well. It seems that with three of you living on the same street, there's always one too many. You decide you're only going to hang with one friend at a time because you're tired of the drama.

Someone in class just said something terrible about your BFF. You quickly jump in to set the record straight. No one is going to say something bad about your friend!

☐ It's Friday and you told one friend she could ride the bus home with you after school, but a better offer has come up. You decide to go with friend number two to the movies instead.

☐ Your friend just got a really bad haircut and she's crying her eyes out. You tell her truthfully that you really loved it longer but she's always adorable in your book. You remind her that it'll grow back.

☐ The girl two doors down just told you her scariest secret last night: She thinks her mom and dad are getting divorced. You can't help yourself. You tell the girls at school during lunch break.

☐ You didn't mean to do it, but you hurt the feelings of one of your classmates. You write her a note to apologize.

Okay, now that you've taken a good look at some fictional scenarios, let's take it up a notch.

Write one real-life scenario where you showed the kind of love that makes a friendship run on a full tank:

. . . .

. . . .

. . . .

. . . .

. . . .

Now, write one scenario where you have to confess that you drained the Love Meter big-time:

. . . .

. . . .

. . . .

. . . .

. . . .

. . . .

If you were to put a great big star on the place where the needle on your Love Meter generally points, where would it be? Mark that spot with a star.

Now, write one idea that can help you be more consistent in operating on full:

. . . .

. . . .

. . . .

. . . .

. . . .

. . . .

Secret Keeper Girl
Girl Gab

Friendship with My Neighbor

On our first SKG date, that awesome SKG-Style Slumber Party, you discovered that at the root of all relationships must be true love. So, this week we begin a quest to discover just what true love looks like. It's not that feeling like butterflies in your tummy. No, it's not that at all! God's Word defines love, and it's going to take us seven dates to really explore his full definition. Along the way, we'll learn how to find new friends, handle the emotions of getting left out, stop jealousy, control your tongue, and honor your parents—and even learn how to be friends with boyz. Best of all, we find all that advice in just one chapter of the Bible: 1 Corinthians 13!

Today, let's just focus on the first three verses.

> *"If I speak with the tongues of men and of angels, but
> do not have love, I have become a noisy gong or a
> clanging cymbal. If I have the gift of prophecy, and
> know all mysteries and all knowledge; and if I have
> all faith, so as to remove mountains, but do not have
> love, I am nothing. And if I give all my possessions
> to feed the poor, and if I surrender my body to be
> burned, but do not have love, it profits me nothing."*
> 1 Corinthians 13:1-3 NASB

According to 1 Corinthians 13:1-3 and our SKG audio teaching today, fill in this blank.

Real love overflows with _____.

It's easy to be consumed with how love shows up in your family and in friendships. But if you have real love in your heart, you'll also love your neighbors. According to our SKG audio teaching, who is your neighbor?

_____.

If you are pursuing true love, you'll find yourself willing to go out and do extraordinary acts of kindness for people you don't even know. You'll be willing to get out from behind your Wii. You'll get off of Facebook. You'll forget the reruns of *Hannah Montana* that you've seen ten times, and you'll go out and act on the love God's put in your heart!

How did you and your mom commit an act of kindness today?
Pretend you're preparing a newspaper article to report on it.
Write your story below and begin with this sentence:

"An act of kindness was committed today at…"

. . . .
Where?
. . . .
When?
. . . .
Who?
. . . .
What?
. . . .

. . . .

Who did you meet along the way? Draw a picture of one to three people you met and then next to the pictures, write how you might pray for them with your mom. What special needs did you notice or did they tell you about?

Now, back to our key Bible verse. Not only does it mention that we need to do acts of kindness, but it says more. Look at it to fill in two more blanks.

If we do anything without _____ *we are* _____.

Hmm? I don't know about you, but I often do acts of kindness to get attention and to be applauded. It's really hard to do them just out of love. That's why today when you were out and about, I asked you to say, "I just want to show God's love in a practical way." Shining the glory on God goes a long way in stretching my heart to love.

There's another thing that helps—praying! You'll end your date tonight by praying. What will you pray about? Go back to your drawings of three people that you met. Write one idea of how you can pray for that person next to each one.

Now, remember to pray over the next few days for the people you met.

One more thing! You can join me in the huge but ultimately completely rewarding goal of memorizing the entire chapter of 1 Corinthians 13. You can start now by learning verses 1-3! I'll be doing it along with you.

Doodle Box!

Friendship with Mean Girlz

Hello, my Secret Keeper Girlfriend! How are you doing with your memorization? Me? I'm doing great. Hold on! Wait just one minute…

There!

I just recited 1 Corinthians 13:1-3 out loud.

Your turn. Say it out loud to your mom. Ask her to say it for you.

Keep working on it. Let's make it a goal to be able to say the whole chapter together. I totally promise that I'm memorizing right along with you.

Okay…on to verses 4-6.

> *"Love is patient and kind; love does not envy or boast;*
> *it is not arrogant or rude. It does not insist on its*

*own way; it is not irritable or resentful; it does not
rejoice at wrongdoing, but rejoices with the truth."*
1 Corinthians 13:4-6

According to 1 Corinthians 13:4-6 and our SKG audio teaching today, fill in this blank.

True love is _____.

Mean Girlz

Did you observe anyone being impatient at the mall today? Who?

· ·

· ·

· ·

· ·

What do you think they did wrong?

· ·

· ·

· ·

· ·

That brings us to an important subject, doesn't it? Sometimes people are really mean. Mean girlz come in all shapes and sizes and test our patience to the max. Here are a few:

Lucy the Leaver-Outer. The leaver-outer is not totally mean to your face, but she makes sure you aren't included in things. She might plan a party and not invite you or someone else in your group of friends. Occasionally, she's not that subtle. Take, for example, when she says: *"This seat is taken!"*

Rule-Setting Ruth. The rule-setter decides who is in and who is out. You never really know who will be her target.

Take this example:

Rule-Setting Ruth: "Hey everyone, we're going to pack our lunch in our Vera Bradley lunch bags tomorrow."

Ruth's target: "But I don't have one."

Rule-Setting Ruth: "Well, everyone else does, so let's do it anyway!"

Jealous Jane. Jealousy creeps in when you or another friend in the group achieves something special. Maybe you got your first A-plus. Jealous Jane often tries to "one-up" you by saying something like this:

"Oh, I got an A-plus on the last test...and the one before that too. I would have had an A-plus on this test, but I helped my aunt move last night and I never got to study, so I only got an A-minus!"

Beatrice the Queen Bee Bully. Beatrice is the meanest of them all and might not be close to you. Most people are afraid that if they get too close to her, they'll be her target. So everyone lets her do her nasty stuff and just tries to steer clear of her cruel remarks like:

"Hey, Banana Bottom! Think you could have a bigger bottom? I could probably pop it with a pin!"

Okay, look back over those four mean-girl options. First, let me ask you to be over-the-top honest. Are you ever one of these girls? If so, put a square around that name. Take a moment to write a prayer of confession to God right here and ask him to help you to control your actions to be more like 1 Corinthians 13:4-6.

. . . .

. . . .

. . . .

. . . .

Now, go back to the list and use a circle to note any types of mean girlz you have to face at school, at church, or in your neighborhood.

How will you respond to that girl or those girls? Well, 1 Corinthians 13:4-6 gives you lots of ideas. Read over it and then rewrite a few ideas of how to respond here.

. . . .

. . . .

. . . .

. . . .

. . . .

. . . .

I want to focus on just one word of wisdom from 1 Corinthians 13. Go back and circle the words "Love is patient." I talked about these three words during your SKG Radio time today. What did I say that the writer of this book of the Bible, Paul, was really saying?

. . . .

. . . .

. . . .

. . . .

. . . .

. . . .

What does it mean to you to be "slow to boil" in friendships?

. . . .

. . . .

. . . .

. . . .

. . . .

Today as you were shopping, you might have begun to feel what "boiling" inside feels like if you started to run out of time. Can you describe it?

. . . .

. . . .

. . . .

. . . .

. . . .

If you'd had all day to spend your money, you wouldn't have felt the same pressure and sense of "boiling." I think that sometimes the reason people are mean is because pressure is building up and too much is expected in a relationship. It's important not to put your friendships under too much pressure. Circle some examples of how *you* might put friendships under pressure.

- Demanding that your friend spend more or at least as much time with you as with anyone else.
- Asking a friend to not talk to certain people you don't like.
- Telling friends to dress or act a certain way.
- Always wanting them at your house.
- Always wanting to be at their house.
- Telling their secrets to other friends.
- Getting them in trouble at school or at home.
- Joining in when other people make fun of them or laugh.
- Nagging them to call you or e-mail you.
- Not including them in conversations.
- Talking about them to someone who doesn't like them.
- Ignoring them when you don't feel like talking.

Now underline any of those things that girls do to you.

Okay. Our goal is to be "slow to boil." To do that, we need to take off some pressure. Can you write one thing you need to do to take some pressure off of friendships where mean girl tendencies might be creeping in?

. . . .

. . . .

. . . .

Okay, practice that one thing until our next date and see if it doesn't make both you and your friend "slow to boil"!

An SKG Bonus!

Truth or Bare Fashion Tests!

Before we set you loose to shop, I have a few modesty tests every single outfit has to pass. I like to call them the SKG Truth or Bare Fashion Tests. If you did the Secret Keeper Girl dates on true beauty, cool fashion, and modesty, you already know them. Review each test and take them as a group.

Test: Raise & Praise

Target question: Am I showing too much belly?

Action: Stand straight up, pretend you're really going for it in worship, and extend your arms in the air for God. Is this exposing a lot of belly? If it is, you may want to find a solution.

Solution: Go to the guys' department and buy a simple ribbed T-shirt or A-line tank top to wear under your funky short shirts, crop tops, or with your trendy low-rider jeans. Layers are a great solution to belly shirts!

Test: Grandpa's Mirror

Target question: How short is too short?

Action: Get in front of a full-length mirror. If you are in shorts, sit cross-legged. If you are in a skirt, sit in a chair with your legs crossed all ladylike. Now, what do you see in that mirror? Okay, pretend that mirror is your grandpa! If you can see undies or lots of thigh, your shorts or skirt is probably too short.

Solution: Buy longer shorts and skirts!

Test: I See London, I See France

Target question: Can you see my underpants?

Action: Bend over and touch your knees. Have a friend or your mom look right at your bottom. Can she see your underpants or the seams in them? How about the color of them? Can she see your actual underwear because your pants are so low? If so, we have a problem!

Solution: Wear white panties with white clothes. If your pants are so tight that you can see the outline of your panties, try buying one size larger. If your pants are too low, throw on one of those guys' tank tops (we call them secret weapons!).

Test: Spring Valley

Target question: Is my shirt too tight?

Action: Before I tell you how to take this test, I should let you know that you might not need it just yet! It all depends on whether God has chosen for you to begin to grow breasts or

not. (And his timing is different for all of us, so be patient!) Maybe you can have your mom take this test! Ask her to place the tips of her fingers together and press into her shirt right in the "valley" between the breasts. Count to three and have her take her fingers away. If her shirt springs back like a mini-trampoline, it's too tight!

Solution: Don't buy clothes based on size. Buy them based on fit. Often you have to go a few sizes larger these days to have a modest fit.

Test: Over & Out

Target question: Is my shirt too low?

Action: Lean forward a little bit. Can you see too much chest skin or future cleavage? If so, your shirt is too low.

Solution: Today's fashions thrive on low-cut shirts. Layering them is usually your only and best remedy. Throw on a little crew-neck T-shirt underneath, and you have a great look!

Doodle Box!

Friendship with My BFF

Welcome back, SKG!

Before we start talking about why we did this date, can I ask you to recite 1 Corinthians 13:1-6?

The memorization for this date is so easy! We're only going to add three little words.

"Love bears all things..."
1 Corinthians 13:7a

✲✲✲

Some versions say it more simply: "Love protects." According to 1 Corinthians 13:7a and our SKG audio teaching today, fill in this blank.

Real love doesn't _____.

Gossip is what happens when you hear a juicy secret from a friend, who heard it from another friend, who may have heard it from someone else, who might have made it up! Simply put, gossip is talking about someone in ways that aren't kind or truthful.

Chances are gossip is floating around your school and neighborhood just like it floats around mine. It might even creep into your church if you're not careful. Sometimes, it's harmless.

"Hey, I heard Jenny's dad has more money than the Jonas Brothers!"

But sometimes it's very hurtful to someone or to a group of people.

"Psst! Did you notice that the girl who sits in the front row of art class smells bad? I heard she hasn't showered in a month!"

Gossip is cruel, but there sure is a lot of it out there! Let's talk about gossip.

Finish the sentences below and then share them with your mom:

The most hurtful thing that anyone has ever said about me was...

. . . .

. . . .

. . . .

. . . .

This made me feel...

. . . .

. . . .

. . . .

If I heard someone spreading gossip or lies about my BFF, I would...

. . . .

. . . .

. . . .

. . . .

. . . .

True love doesn't gossip. Remember from our teaching that I told you that the New Testament of the Bible is written in which language?

Hebrew   Swahili   Greek   Martian

It's so much clearer sometimes when we can just hear what God was trying to say to us in Greek, so remember with me what he was really saying when he told us that love protects.

The original Greek wording actually said "Love covers in silence"! What a great picture for friendship this creates. The next time you hear something from your friend or about her, make sure you "cover" her "in silence"! Simply put, keep her secrets secret.

When your friend tells you something private, it is one of the highest compliments you can get. She is saying, "I trust you!" Do you really want to lose that?

No way!

Cover your friend in silence!

There's only one really big exception to the rule of covering your friends in silence: If your friend is in danger, you need to tell an adult. *But not your other friends!*

Doodle Box!

Friendship with My Parents

Welcome back, SKG!

You should have a very special guest on your SKG date today! Let's start our Girl…er, Girl *and* Guy Gab right. Recite 1 Corinthians 13:1-7a for your favorite guy!

We're going to add just a little bit more of verse 7 today. In fact, it's so short that we're going to include what you learned on the last date.

"Love bears all things, believes all things…"
1 Corinthians 13:7a

You can believe in something if it is true. When there is someone in your life you can always believe, it is easy to trust them. What this verse is really saying is that we can trust someone who loves us. According to 1 Corinthians 13:7a and our SKG audio teaching today, fill in this blank.

True love _____.

There's a very old song that kids used to learn. It goes like this:

Trust and obey,
For there's no other way
To be happy in Jesus,
But to trust and obey.

It's not going to make it to iTunes anytime soon, but it teaches us a good truth. Trusting really is obedience. It's like *trust* and *obedience* are married to each other. You can't trust someone without obeying them or favoring their opinion and advice. Ugh! That's so hard, isn't it?

This is one of the greatest and hardest ways to show true love. Jesus even said, "If you obey my commands, you will remain in my love" (John 15:10 GNT). We show our love to God through trust and obedience.

We trust and obey God by trusting and obeying those he's put in authority over us. He's given you parents and other adults in your life to guide you toward him. We're going to spend this date exploring trust by playing a fun game.

The Question Box

Your Girl Gab for this date was to play "The Box of Questions" game on the next two pages. Did you like it? What are some of your favorite memories from the game? Write a few here.

1.

2.

3.

4.

5.

Doodle Box!

The Box of Questions for Date #5:

Friendship with My Parents

Dad: "What makes you trust your daughter? What qualities in her do you see that make you feel she'll make good decisions when you are not around?"

Mom: "What makes you trust your husband? Tell your daughter why you feel that his wisdom and advice can be trusted."

Daughter: "How does it make you feel when your mom or dad trusts you to do something new that you've never done before? Maybe you can start by remembering the last time that happened. Maybe you got to ride your bike further than before or go on a trip without your family."

Dad: "It's really important that your daughter trusts you to guide her concerning boys. How do you want to see your daughter interacting with them at her age?"

Mom: "When you were young was there ever a time when you broke your parents' trust? If so, how did you earn it back?"

Daughter: "Other than your mom and dad, who is someone older and wiser in your life that you would trust—that is, you'd not only tell them your secrets, but you'd obey their advice—and why?"

Dad: "Which of your daughter's friends do you trust most to help her make good decisions in life, and why?"

Mom: "Who is your best friend or an accountability partner? Tell your daughter what it is like to have a friend who knows everything about you and whom you trust to keep your secrets! Tell her about a time when you 'obeyed' her advice."

Daughter: "Other than trustworthiness, what are some of the qualities of love that you see in your dad?" (We've learned about acts of kindness, being patient, and not gossiping. You might select one of these and tell your dad how you see him live that out in his life!)

Dad: "What does it feel like to trust and obey God? Tell your daughter about a time when this was difficult for you, but you learned that you can trust him. Explain to her that even when other people fail her—and all humans may—God can always be trusted."

Friendship with My Siblings

Hello, my friend! I hope you just had a really special time with a brother, sister, or mentor in your life. Did you?

Let's start our Girl Gab time by reciting your memory verse for them. Recite out loud 1 Corinthians 13:1-7b!

Now let's add the rest of verse 7.

> *"Love bears all things, believes all things,*
> *hopes all things, endures all things."*
> 1 Corinthians 13:7

According to 1 Corinthians 13:7 and our SKG teaching today, fill in this blank.

True love _____.

What do you think it means to hope? Write your answer below.

. . . .

. . . .

. . . .

. . . .

The dictionary says that hope is "the feeling that what is wanted can be had"! It means that you believe good things are going to happen in the future. It doesn't mean you believe that everything is just perfect right now.

Do you ever find that your sibling barges into your space without knocking? Or maybe he or she deliberately tries to annoy you with stupid jokes. That's sort of how it works with brothers and sisters, but under all of that there should be "true love" which includes hope for each other.

Hold that thought!

Let's take a quick test to see how well you know your sibling. Circle choices on both sides—one side for you and one for your sibling.

Which Do You Like Better?

You	Me
PB and J or grilled cheese	PB and J or grilled cheese
Dogs or cats	Dogs or cats
Sports events or musicals	Sports events or musicals
A beach vacation or camping in the woods	A beach vacation or camping in the woods
Pants or skirts	Pants or skirts
Board games or movies	Board games or movies
Winter or summer	Winter or summer
Pancakes or scrambled eggs	Pancakes or scrambled eggs
Snickerdoodles or chocolate chip cookies	Snickerdoodles or chocolate chip cookies
Math or English	Math or English

Okay, now compare. How well do you and your sibling actually know each other? If you did really well, congratulations! You must be spending some time together getting to know each other. Good job.

If you didn't know how to answer these questions at all, you are either 1) not spending enough time together or 2) in serious relationship trouble!

Does it matter if we know each other's favorites? Sure it does. It shows how much we take time to get outside of our own selfish desires to be concerned about our brother or sister. Do you know what he or she hopes to be when they grow up? Do you know how well your sibling is doing in school and what hopes he or she has to improve or stay on course?

When we know someone, it creates the knowledge we need to have hope for them.

What are three things that you hope for your brother or sister? Maybe you are still praying for your sibling's salvation. Perhaps you hope he or she can be a teacher someday because that's what he or she wants. Write three things below.

1.

2.

3.

Share your list with your sibling and let him or her share with you his or her hope for you.

An SKG Extra

Log on to www.secretkeepergirl.com to see how my daughters, Lexi and Autumn, got to know each other! It wasn't easy! They did not speak the same language...literally. Lexi speaks English and, at the time, Autumn only spoke Mandarin. (We adopted Autumn when both of the girls were 13, and they met for the first time in Nanchang, China!) But God has overcome every obstacle for them to "hope" the best for each other. Check out these fun videos for more details.

Friendship with God

Where does real love come from? It's really easy to be emotional and girly and think that it comes from Prince Charming. We tend to believe that from a very young age. You could go your whole life kissing lots of frogs with that mentality and never really find true love. No, love doesn't come from some sort of romantic relationship. Today we'll explore the source of true love.

But first...how's that memorization coming?

Recite 1 Corinthians 13:1-7 out loud.

Keep working on it. Today we are going to add a huge chunk! You can do it. You've had it very, very easy for the last few dates.

"Love never ends. As for prophecies, they will pass away;
as for tongues, they will cease; as for knowledge,
it will pass away. For we know in part and we prophesy
in part, but when the perfect comes, the partial will pass
away. When I was a child, I spoke like a child,

*I thought like a child, I reasoned like a child. When
I became a man, I gave up childish ways."*
1 Corinthians 13:8-11

According to 1 Corinthians 13:8-11 and our SKG audio teaching today, fill in this blank.

Real love _____.

One version of the Bible says it this way: "Love never fails." I bet your friends have failed you. Some may have even stopped loving you altogether. I bet your teachers have disappointed you at times. Humans are imperfect and they will fail. Can you recall a time when you felt like someone who was supposed to love you disappointed you? Write about it below.

· ·

· ·

· ·

· ·

That hurt, didn't it? Of course it did! You know why? Read the verse below:

"What is desired in a man is steadfast love,
and a poor man is better than a liar."
Proverbs 19:22

The word "steadfast" means "unfailing." God created us to desire unfailing love. We are lying if we don't admit it. It's never wrong to feel hurt when we don't feel loved. It's a natural response, but if you spend all of your life trying to focus on love from humans, you're bound to feel hurt a whole lot. So, let's see if we can get you started in a better direction.

It's like when your mom tried to plug in two things that didn't belong together. What happened?

. . . .

. . . .

. . . .

. . . .

There was no power in it.

Well, there's only one source of unfailing love and you've got to plug into it every day, my Secret Keeper Girl. Read the verses below and circle the only source of true, unfailing love, or stead-fast love.

*"Let me hear in the morning of your steadfast love,
for in you I trust. Make me know the way I should go,
for to you I lift up my soul. Deliver me…O Lord!
I have fled to you for refuge!"*
Psalm 143:8-9

*"I have trusted in your steadfast love;
my heart shall rejoice in your salvation.
I will sing to the Lord."*
Psalm 13:5-6a

*"We have thought on your steadfast love,
O God, in the midst of your temple."*
Psalm 48:9

There is only one source of unfailing or steadfast love, and it is God. You've got to "plug in" to him every day. Can you think of some ways that you can "plug in" to God? Write them below.

. . . .

. . . .

. . . .

. . . .

One of the best ways to "plug in" to God is to spend time with him every day. I want to challenge you to spend time with him regularly for the next two weeks. Will you sign my True Love Contract to make a commitment to do that?

The True Love Contract

Here's how it works.

1. Challenge yourself to spend time "plugging in" to God every day. I want you to do this for the next two weeks, for five out of seven days a week. (I'm giving you some days off!) To make it fun, put something on the line. For example, if you miss more than two days in a week, you might promise your mom that you'll organize her underwear drawer. (Ew! Yuck!) She might agree to walk the dog for you if she misses. It'll be fun to check up on each other. Keep it fun and light!

2. Agree to the challenge by signing the True Love Contract on page 195. When you get home you can tape it to your mirror or somewhere in your bedroom where you can see it every day.

To make it easy, this book includes ten mini-devotions (see page 129) written by me and my Bod Squad—Suzy, Janet, and Chizzy. (They also helped me write a great fiction series that you should check out! Go to www.secretkeepergirl.com.)

Why not try one of the devos out right now?

Doodle Box!

TLC
True Love Contract

"Let me hear in the morning of your steadfast love,
for in you I trust. Make me know the way I should go,
for to you I lift up my soul. Deliver me…O Lord!
I have fled to you for refuge!"
Psalm 143:8-9

❋❋❋

Did I Spend Time "Plugging In" to God Today?

I, _____, will attempt to spend time "plugging in" to God through quiet prayer and Bible reading during the next two weeks. I will commit to doing this for five out of every seven days. If I miss more than two days a week, I will

. . . .

. . . .

. . . .

. . . .

for Mom.

Signed: _____

Dated: _____

Friendship with Boyz

So, here we are in our final week. How's your memorization? Why not try saying what you have memorized so far? Ready for our final verses?

"Now we see in a mirror dimly,
but then face to face. Now I know in part;
then I shall know fully, even as I have been fully known.
So now faith, hope, and love abide, these three;
but the greatest of these is love."
1 Corinthians 13:12-13

According to this verse and our SKG audio teaching, finish this sentence.

Love _____ the one it loves.

Okay, crazy quiz time. Fast-forward with me to your wedding day. Here you are! Imagine with me…what is it like? What dress are you wearing? What kind of flowers are you carrying? Who is there with you? Maybe you've already dreamed about this day just a little bit. Can you dream on paper? Write two things about your wedding day that you hope for.

1.

2.

Secret Keeper Girl, our last Girl Gab is very, very deep. Buckle up! The ride may be bumpy. We're going to talk about boyz!

Read the two verses below and circle the word that is similar.

> *"Adam knew Eve."*
> *Genesis 4:1a* NKJV

> *"Be still, and know that I am God."*
> *Psalm 46:10*

Both words—"knew" and "know"—actually mean "to know, to be known, to be deeply respected" in the original Bible language.

These verses are from the Old Testament—not the New, which is written in Greek. Any idea what language the Old Testament is written in? Give it a guess.

_____

Anyway, back to our words: "knew" and "know." They're really talking about two precious and holy relationships. Which two relationships are mentioned in these verses? Circle two.

God and man

Brothers and sisters

Moms and daughters

Husbands and wives

That's right—the relationship between God and man *and* the relationship between husband and wife both get this special, holy word...to "know"! All through the Bible, God uses the same word to talk about his relationship with us *and* a husband's relationship with his wife. What does that tell you about a relationship between a husband and a wife?

. . . .

. . . .

. . . .

. . . .

If God wants you to get married someday, nothing will get in the way. But just like you and I are only supposed to worship one God, we need only one special relationship with a guy. The world may tell you that you need dozens and dozens of boyfriends by the time you are 16, but that's not God's desire for you. He wants you to have just one special man in your life, and it's not time just yet!

Do you feel any pressure to have a boyfriend or to be boy-crazy?

. . . .

. . . .

. . . .

. . . .

If yes, what do you think causes that pressure?

. . . .

. . . .

. . . .

. . . .

Now, back to our special verse in 1 Corinthians. It says, "Now I know in part." This sounds familiar. "Know"! What does the word "know" mean again?

. . . .

. . . .

. . . .

. . . .

In the New Testament, this word is used again to describe two relationships. Which two do you think? Write them below.

. . . .

. . . .

. . . .

. . . .

That's right! Our relationship with God. And our relationship with our future husbands. This earthly love of husband and wife is so special that it should be set apart to be pure and special. What can you do right now to set yourself apart from the boy-crazy world you live in?

. . . .

. . . .

. . . .

. . . .

Doodle Box!

Notes

1. "National Survey Shatters Perception of 'Tween' Girls," *Business Wire*, October 10, 2003; retrieved July 26, 2007, www.highbeam.com.

2. Joshua Mann, Joe S. McIlhaney Jr., and Curtis C. Stine, *Building Healthy Futures* (Austin, TX: Medical Institute for Sexual Health, 2000).

3. Jeffrey Zaslow, "Daddy's Girl, Interrupted: In a World of Date Rape, Drugs and Risque Clothing, These Are Precarious Times for Fathers," *Chicago Sun-Times*, November 19, 2003; retrieved July 26, 2007, www.highbeam.com.

4. "National Survey Shatters Perception of 'Tween' Girls."

5. "National Survey Shatters Perception of 'Tween' Girls."

6. "Should parents decide if you can—or can't be friends with someone?" *Discovery Girls*, December/January 2008, 20.

7. www.msnbc.msn.com/id/24315977/ns/nbcnightlynews/t/teen-text-lingo-decoded/#.UCbI70TkD-Y; retrieved January 2008. Also see the parent texting guide release from AT&T.

8. Zaslow.

9. Patricia L. East, Emily J. Horn, and Barbara T. Reyes, "Association Between Adolescent Pregnancy and a Family History of Teenage Births," *Perspectives on Sexual and Reproductive Health*, June 2, 2007; retrieved January 17, 2008, highbeam.com.

10. Laurie Chassin, Eileen Leuthe, Ryan S. Trim, "Sibling influence on alcohol use in a young adult, high risk sample," *Journal of Studies on Alcohol*, May 1, 2006; retrieved January 17, 2008, highbeam.com.

11. Beth Moore, *Praying God's Word* (Nashville, TN: Broadman and Holman Publishers, 2000), 75.

12. Lynn Neary, "Media, Sex and Talking To Teens," *Talk of the Nation* (NPR), transcript from August 7, 2006; retrieved July 26, 2007, www.highbeam.com.

13. Julia Fein Azoulay, "The Changing Scene of the American Tween," *Children's Business*, March 1, 2003; retrieved August 30, 2012, www.highbeam.com.

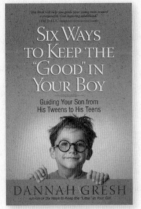

SIX WAYS TO KEEP THE "GOOD" IN YOUR BOY
Guiding Your Son from His Tweens to His Teens

> *"This book will help you guide your
> young man toward a purposeful,
> God-honoring adulthood."*
>
> JIM DALY
> PRESIDENT, FOCUS ON THE FAMILY

God created boys to become men who are good—acting for the sake of others and having others' interests at heart, especially as husbands and fathers. As a mom, you have a unique role in equipping your son to embrace this call from God...and stand against a culture that wants to strip him of his masculinity.

Bestselling author Dannah Gresh blends thorough analysis of the latest research and trends that can impact your son—including porn, aggressive girls, and video games gone overboard—with positive, practical advice any mom can use effectively to help guide her son toward "good" during the vital ages of 8 to 12. Dannah shows you

- why a boy needs to play outside
- how reading good books makes him a leader
- what role a mom plays in his entrance into manhood
- tips to keep him unplugged from impurity

----
*With special insights for dads from Bob Gresh
and for single moms from Angela Thomas*

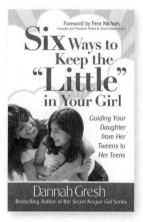

SIX WAYS TO KEEP THE "LITTLE" IN YOUR GIRL

Guiding Your Daughter from Her Tweens to Her Teens

Today's world pressures girls to act older than they are when they're not ready for it. How can you help your tween daughter navigate the stormy waters of boy-craziness, modesty, body image, media, Internet safety, and more?

Dannah Gresh shares six easy ways to help your daughter grow up to be confident, emotionally healthy, and strong in her faith. In a warm and transparent style, Dannah shows you how to

- help your daughter celebrate her body in a healthy way
- unbrand her when the world tries to buy and sell her
- unplug her from a plugged-in world
- dream with her about her future

> *"A practical, biblically based resource to navigate the rapids of raising a tween girl...Even better, this book is fun to read—more like eating dark chocolate than eating broccoli. Enjoy!"*
>
> DR. JULI SLATTERY
> FAMILY PSYCHOLOGIST, FOCUS ON THE FAMILY

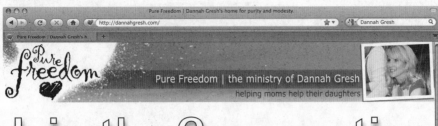